Dracones Loquí

Dracones Loqui

Copyright © 2025 Ravynne Phelan

All rights reserved. Other than for personal use, no part of these cards or this book may be reproduced in any way, in whole or part, without the written consent of the copyright holder or publisher. This publication is intended for spiritual and emotional guidance only. The content is not intended to replace medical assistance or treatment. The views and opinions expressed by the author, both within and outside of this publication, do not necessarily reflect the views of the publisher.

Published by Blue Angel Publishing®
10 Trafford Court, Wheelers Hill,
Victoria, Australia 3150
E-mail: info@blueangelonline.com
Website: www.blueangelonline.com

Edited by Peter Loupelis and Jules Sutherland

Blue Angel is a registered trademark of Blue Angel Gallery Pty Ltd.

ISBN: 978-1-922574-26-8

Ravynne Phelan
Dracones Loquí

Table of Contents

Author's Note..................................8
"Behold! The Dragons Speak"................11
How To Use the Cards....................14
Card Spreads..............................16

Card Meanings

Beginning....................................**20**
Breathe......................................**23**
Burden.......................................**25**
Centre.......................................**27**
Chaos..**30**
Choice.......................................**32**
Communicate............................**35**
Conflict......................................**37**
Connection................................**40**

Create	**43**
Dance	**45**
Dichotomy	**47**
Direction	**50**
Fears	**52**
Flow	**54**
Focus	**56**
Forewarning	**59**
Fulfilment	**61**
Give and Receive	**64**
Gratitude	**66**
Guide	**69**
Hope	**71**
Intimacy	**73**
Journey	**76**
Leap	**78**
Learn	**80**
Love	**83**
Magic	**85**
Message	**87**
Mind	**90**
Mourn	**92**
Nourish	**95**
Order	**97**
Passion	**100**

Power	**102**
Prayer	**104**
Rest	**107**
Ripples	**109**
Rituals	**111**
Scream	**114**
See	**116**
Self	**119**
Shelter	**121**
Soar	**124**
Spirit	**126**
Strength	**128**
Structure	**130**
Suffering	**133**
Temple	**135**
Time	**138**
Transcend	**140**
Treasure	**142**
Trinity	**144**
Truth	**146**
Acknowledgements	**151**
About the Creator	**153**

This is for my dragons
who have watched over me,
loved me,
and kept me safe.

Author's Note

• • •

DEAR SEEKER,

It is with immense joy, gratitude, and relief that I present to you *Dracones Loqui* ('Dragons Speak'). This deck has been a labour of love, born from a singular moment of deep connection to the mystical realms and a profound reverence for the wisdom of dragons.

In crafting this deck, my intention was to create a sacred space — a sanctuary where seekers like you can commune with the celestial guardians known as Lux, Terra, and Umbra. These mighty dragons embody the essence of the universe, with each individual personality offering a unique perspective, guidance, and love.

This deck offers options and embraces diversity in perspectives.

As you journey through the cards of this deck, may you feel the gentle embrace of Lux's compassionate light, guiding you with love and understanding. May you find grounding and stability in Terra's earthly wisdom as you navigate the practicalities of life with grace and resilience. And may you embrace the transformative power of Umbra's tough love, facing your shadows with courage and emerging stronger and more radiant than ever before.

Rest assured, dear seeker, you are never alone on this journey. The dragons, with their wings outstretched to shield you from life's storms, their hearts open wide to embrace you with unwavering love, and their voices always present to guide you, are your steadfast companions on the path of enlightenment.

May *Dracones Loqui* be a source of inspiration, guidance, and empowerment on your quest for truth, healing, and self-discovery.

With much love and gratitude,
Ravynne

"Behold! The Dragons Speak"

Welcome, seeker, to the realm of Dracones Loqui — *where dreams take flight, where realities intertwine, and where the whispers of the Divine echo through the corridors of eternity.*

In a realm where dreams and reality intertwine, there exists a temple of incredible beauty and mystery. Perched atop a mountain peak so high that it touches heaven, this sanctuary stands as a gateway between mortals and the Divine.

Within the hallowed halls of this celestial refuge resides a guardian of an extraordinary nature — a dragon who is not one but three. Three cosmic dragons, their scales ablaze with the brilliance of a million stars, their breath carrying the very essence of creation. Known by the names of Lux, Terra, and Umbra, they are not mere creatures of flesh and bone but embodiments of cosmic forces, bearers of ancient knowledge, and stewards of the balance that sustains the universe.

Lux

'The Shining One'—a creature of celestial grace—stands as a beacon of light amidst the darkness. Their presence is like a warm embrace, and their voice is a symphony of compassion and understanding that reverberates through the fabric of existence. To encounter Lux is to bask in the gentle glow of unconditional love, find solace in the embrace of cosmic empathy, and witness the beauty that resides within the depths of the soul.

Terra

'The Earthy One' is a passionate advocate for the wild and the green. Their gaze is steady, their demeanour resolute, their wisdom as ancient as the stones upon which they stand. Terra embodies the strength and resilience of the natural world, a testament to the enduring power of simplicity, authenticity, and connection to the land. To heed Terra's counsel is to walk the path of groundedness, to draw strength from the rhythms of nature, and to find wisdom in the whispers of the wind and the song of the soil. She is the mother and the giver of practical advice and instruction.

Umbra

'The Shadowy One' is shrouded in the mysteries of the night, their presence cloaked in shadows as deep as the void between stars. Their eyes pierce through illusions, their words cutting through the veil of falsehood with the precision of a blade forged in the fires of truth. Umbra embodies the harsh realities of existence, their voice a reminder of the inevitability of change, the necessity of facing one's fears, and the transformative power of embracing the darkness within. To heed Umbra's guidance is to confront the shadows that lurk within the depths of the soul, to emerge from the crucible of adversity stronger, wiser, and more resilient than ever before.

Together, Lux, Terra, and Umbra watch over humanity from their celestial abode, their gaze spanning the breadth of time and space, their hearts ever open to those who seek their guidance. Through the ages, they have whispered in the minds of those whose hearts beat with the rhythm of the dragons, offering solace to the weary, wisdom to the seekers, and light to those lost in the darkness.

It is within this sacred context that the oracle *Dracones Loqui* was conceived — a testament to the enduring bond between mortals and the Divine, a conduit through which seekers may commune with the celestial guardians who watch over them. Each card within this sacred deck serves as a portal to the realm of Lux, Terra, and Umbra, offering glimpses of their timeless wisdom, their boundless love, and their unwavering guidance.

As you embark upon your journey, know that you are not alone. Lux, Terra, and Umbra stand as your guides, your protectors, and your companions. May their wisdom illuminate your journey, may their presence comfort your soul, and may their guidance lead you ever closer to the truth that dwells within.

How To Use the Cards

Dracones Loqui is a tool for self-reflection, guidance, and spiritual exploration. Whether used for daily inspiration, deep soul-searching, or connecting with higher realms of consciousness, this deck is a valuable companion on your journey of self-discovery and personal growth.

Below are several suggestions for using the deck:

1. **Daily Guidance:** Start your day by drawing a card from the deck. Take a moment to meditate on the imagery and message of the card. Consider how it applies to your current circumstances or what lessons it may hold for the day ahead.

2. **Affirmations:** Use the affirmations offered with each card to heal and reinforce positive thoughts and emotions.

3. **Journalling:** Keep a journal dedicated to your interactions with the deck. Write down the cards you draw, your initial impressions, and any insights or reflections that arise during your contemplation. Over time, you may notice patterns or recurring themes in your readings.

4. **Intention Setting:** Before drawing a card, set an intention or ask a specific question. Focus your thoughts on what you hope to gain clarity or guidance on. This can help you receive more targeted and relevant messages from the deck.

5. **Creative Visualisation:** Choose a card that resonates with you and visualise yourself embodying the qualities or energies depicted in the imagery and messages. Imagine yourself surrounded by the colours, symbols, and sensations the card elicits, allowing its message to sink deep into your subconscious mind.

Card Spreads

Adjust these spreads as needed to better suit your intentions or the specific questions you have in mind. The flexibility of these layouts allows you to tailor them to your preferences and explore the depths of your consciousness with the guidance of the *Dracones Loqui*.

The first three spreads allow you to dive deep into the energies and messages of Lux, Terra, or Umbra individually, providing focused guidance and insights tailored to your specific needs and intentions. The final spread blends all three energies into a single reading.

Radiant Blessings Spread

Card 1 (Lux): Inner Light & Guidance — This card reflects the inner light and guidance that is within you, offering affirmations of love and empowerment.

Card 2 (Lux): Divine Love & Compassion — This card emphasises the presence of divine love and compassion in your life, encouraging you to extend kindness and empathy to yourself and others.

Card 3 (Lux): Spiritual Connection & Enlightenment — This card offers insights into deepening your spiritual connection and seeking enlightenment, reminding you of the limitless potential within your soul.

Earth Wisdom Spread

Card 1 (Terra): Grounding & Stability — This card provides guidance on grounding yourself in the present moment and finding stability amidst change. It offers practical instructions for nurturing your connection to the earth.

Card 2 (Terra): Environmental Awareness & Stewardship — This card highlights the importance of environmental awareness and stewardship, offering messages related to conservation and sustainability.

Card 3 (Terra): Natural Cycles & Harmony — This card reflects on the natural cycles of life and the harmony found in the rhythms of nature, encouraging you to align with the flow of the earth for greater balance and wellbeing.

Shadow's Insight Spread

Card 1 (Umbra): Facing Truths & Shadow Work — This card encourages confronting your shadows and facing truths with courage and compassion. It offers insights into areas of your life that may require healing or transformation.

Card 2 (Umbra): Tough Love & Growth — This card offers tough love and honest reflections on challenges or obstacles, reminding you of the strength and resilience within you.

Card 3 (Umbra): Embracing Change & Transformation — This card signifies the transformative power of embracing change and the journey of self-discovery and personal growth.

The Dragons' Guidance Spread

The following spread offers a comprehensive blend of guidance, wisdom, and empowerment from Lux, Terra, and Umbra, along with an affirmation to uplift and inspire you on your journey. It encourages you to embrace the full spectrum of energies and insights, empowering you to navigate life's challenges with courage, resilience, and grace.

Card 1 (Lux): Illumination — This card offers empathy and understanding to illuminate your path.

Card 2 (Terra): Motherly Love — This card provides practical instructions and nature messages from Terra, wrapped up in a whole lot of motherly love.

Card 3 (Umbra): Hard Truths — This card reveals hard truths and insights from Umbra, tempered with compassion and love.

Affirmation Card: Inner Strength & Empowerment — this is an affirmation of inner strength and empowerment to provide a healing focus.

Card Meanings

Beginning

Affirmation

In every beginning lies the infinite potential for growth, discovery, and transformation. Today, I embrace the beauty of fresh starts, trusting in my ability to navigate new paths with courage, clarity, and resilience. With each step forward, I am guided by the light of possibility, knowing that every beginning is a doorway to a brighter tomorrow.

Lux Shines

Radiant soul, seek the stillness within, for there lies your true power. Just as I find serenity amidst the swirling galaxies, you must find your centre amidst life's chaos. Still your mind and address the worries that have you fretting about the past and future instead of enjoying the present.

Radiant soul, heed the wisdom of the light. This moment is imbued with potential if you choose to believe in it. It could be a moment of profound joy, hope, or opportunity. Within the boundless Void, a wondrous weaving of time waits for you to conceive it. Beloved child of the dragon, you possess the key to its manifestation and what this moment will become.

Unleash your inner light and breathe life into your dreams. Make them real. As the child of dragons, the time has come to claim your celestial wings and begin a soaring journey into the most creative phase of your existence. Embrace your limitless potential by being present and shaping your reality. Guided by the divine light that dwells within your soul, embark upon a glorious flight into the dawning of your destiny.

Terra Speaks

Little dragon, this moment holds a chance for transformation and progress. Seek fertile ground, whether right where you stand or in a place you've yet to explore. Once found, plant the seeds of newfound knowledge and growth that live within your heart and mind. Set your intentions and focus clearly on your goals.

Clear away the obstacles of doubt, distractions, and discord. Plant your seeds deep in the nurturing darkness and nourish them. Let the light of passion and curiosity provide warmth. Take care to protect these seeds; do all that's necessary to ensure their growth.

Watch as your objectives take root and flourish, twining themselves into the fabric of your journey. Seize this opportunity with diligence and care, for it holds great potential.

Umbra Growls

Ahh, human, your very nature has you clinging to the familiar like moss to stone. Change is the crucible of growth and some things must end to make way for new—

and better—beginnings. The beginnings may place you on a path that will test the very essence of your being. Such is life. But you are stronger and more resilient than you believe. You have so much potential and power if only you would cease your fretting and unshackle yourself from fear's grip. The unknown future is exactly that — unknown. The change that comes is rarely as dire and dark as you imagined, so why do you inflict so much suffering upon yourself in the present?

Yes, human, change comes with a price for good or ill, but it doesn't always have to be paid in blood and misery. Let go and allow life to unfold. Everything happens as it is meant to.

Remember that in the chaos lie the seeds of transformation, waiting to sprout. Don't allow your unwillingness to let things end prevent something new and beautiful from growing in the decay.

Breathe

Affirmation

I am anchored in the rhythm of my breath, finding solace in its gentle ebb and flow. With each inhale, I welcome peace and clarity into my being. With each exhale, I release tension, doubt, and fear. In the simple act of breathing, I find a sanctuary of calm and renewal. Today, I embrace the power of my breath to centre myself, to awaken my spirit, and to navigate life's journey with grace and ease.

Lux Shines

Bright soul, behold the boundless majesty of the Source of All. It weaves an infinite tapestry, transcending all dimensions with infinite ease and grace. Gaze upon the celestial tapestry and realise that your perception is but a shard of a greater truth. All That Is emanates from the cosmic breath of the Void — the Source of All. Close thy earthly eyes, bright soul, and draw the Divine into your being. With each exhale, relinquish the chains that tether your soul. As you breathe, envision ethereal wings lifting your spirit toward the astral realms. Surrender your fears to the boundless cosmos, and let your imagination unfurl amidst the order and chaos of the heavens, where inspiration flourishes eternally.

Terra Speaks

The air you breathe in nourishes all within you, little dragon. To thrive, embrace the breath of air, and understand it's more than mere respiration; it's a communion with the earth's energy — Gaia's energy. Seek stillness beneath a tree-friend, and inhale deeply, for in that inhalation, you take in its healing essence and calm will imbue your body, mind, and spirit.

Remember, what you take sustains you, and what you give sustains the world. So, in your breath, find unity with the divine being who is your earthly mother and home.

Umbra Growls

Human, cease your mindless haste. You rush through your existence with nary a pause, attempting multiple feats at once. Fretful and restless, you force change and growth when time and patience are required. Afraid of missing out, you suffocate your aspirations, even stifling the growth you've forced. Self-sabotage. Life, be it mundane or divine, needs room to inhale and expand.

Observe your breath also, human. Shallow inhalations will not nourish your body, intellect, or soul. Air embodies vitality and vigour. March forth with determination and embrace the art of deep breathing in both mind and body.

Burden

Affirmation

I release the weight of burdens that no longer serve me, freeing myself to embrace the lightness of being. With each exhale, I release the grip of worry and doubt, allowing space for peace and clarity to flow within. I trust in my strength to overcome challenges and to transform burdens into opportunities for growth and resilience. Today, I choose to carry only what is necessary for my journey, leaving behind the rest to pave the way for a brighter tomorrow.

Lux Shines

Oh, bright soul, understand that while your existence is but a strand in the cosmic tapestry, it is woven with purpose. Sometimes, your role may seem insignificant, while it shall be grand and transformative in others.

Understand that, despite your noblest intentions, you may inadvertently inflict pain upon others. Hold their tears and anguish as a sacred burden. Let tears and sorrows become lessons that increase your wisdom and empathy. Embrace the role of catalyst, for in endings, new beginnings are birthed, and change is the heartbeat of the universe. Tears may flow, but they will wash away the veils that conceal inner light, reason, and purpose. Embrace the truth that, like the Divine itself, you are both creation and destruction. The former is your joy. The latter is your burden.

Terra Speaks

As you move through life, little dragon, heed this ancient truth: burdens too heavy breed exhaustion, quenching the fire of appreciation for your toils. They kindle impatience, sow resentment, and drag upon your senses. In this state, the wellspring of compassion and kindness often runs dry.

The time has come to tend to the strains that weigh upon your senses. Seek equilibrium in work and play, the mundane and magical. Prioritise your responsibilities. Let go of those that are not yours to carry.

Today, attend only to the essentials and let your spirit flourish through self-nurturing. The rest can wait until a new day begins.

Umbra Growls

Ah, human, your burden grows heavier with each passing day. Why do you continue to carry the weight of countless tasks upon your shoulders, forsaking delight and mirth for drudgery? Stop being so stubborn. Cease this folly of thinking. You alone hold mastery over every endeavour. Let go of your need to control every outcome and entrust others to share your load. 'Ere you crumble beneath this relentless toil, heed this truth: it does not make you weak to delegate or redistribute the load, especially when failure and disappointment lurk in a solitary struggle. Pride will be your downfall if you persist in saying no to any offer of aid. In unity, strength is forged, and together, you shall conquer any trial.

Centre

Affirmation
At my centre, I find serenity and strength. Anchored in this calm space, I am aligned with my true essence. Like a steady flame, my centre radiates clarity and purpose, guiding me through life's twists and turns. I return to this inner sanctuary with each breath, embracing balance and harmony. Today, I honour the power of my centre, knowing it holds the key to my resilience and inner peace.

Lux Shines
Bright soul, seek the stillness within, for there lies your true power. Just as I find serenity amidst the swirling galaxies, you must find your centre amidst life's chaos. Still your mind and address the worries that have you fretting about the ebb and flow of time. Know that you are a part

of the grand design. You stand at the centre of your reality, a shining star within the universe. Trust in your purpose and intuition, for they are the whispers of the Divine. In stillness, you shall find clarity, strength, and the wisdom to navigate the constellations on your journey. May your path be as magnificent as the galaxies themselves.

Terra Speaks

Little dragon … picture roots anchoring you deep into Gaia's core. Breathe in slowly and let Gaia's strength infuse you. Embrace solitude in nature, for it is your sanctuary. Trust your instincts, for they are your inner compass. Shed worries like old scales, for they weigh you down. Live in the present for the past is over, and the future is a mystery. Cultivate gratitude, for like precious gems, it will enrich your soul. Understand that life's storms will come, but like a mountain, you stand resilient. Seek harmony with your surroundings, for you are part of this vast ecosystem. From your centred place, feel your connection to all that was, All That Is, and all that will be, and remember that life is an ongoing journey with many destinations, not just one.

Umbra Growls

Human, your current chaotic existence is a reckless dance that will take you into the abyss. Centre yourself, for you are like a candle that stands in rising flood waters. By not creating a temple upon high to shelter your inner spark, you leave yourself vulnerable. In times of turmoil, do your best to create a place of calm, or risk being forever blown about in the tempest.

Learn to find solace in silence. Embrace solitude to explore the thoughts within your mind and how they affect or influence your peace of mind. Understand that the external distractions you fill your life with blind you to your purpose. It is time to delve into the void within and confront your shadows. You will emerge stronger. The more you learn, the more you can use the knowledge to feed your inner spark. Let it become a temple fire that burns like a beacon. Let it become a place of power where your mind returns when you are feeling lost and confused.

Time, like an elusive wisp, will slip through your fingers if you do not learn to create order within the chaos. Let your resolve and dedication be unwavering or be forever lost in a storm of procrastination and regret.

And, human, when you succeed and that inner spark becomes a bonfire, don't allow anyone to have you believe you shine too bright. Be glorious, and shine like the sun.

Chaos

Affirmation

In the midst of chaos, I remain grounded and resilient. Like an ancient oak in a storm, I stand firm in my truth and inner calm. Chaos is an opportunity for growth and transformation, and I navigate its challenges with courage and clarity. In moments of chaos, I find strength and wisdom, emerging stronger and wiser. Chaos is a catalyst for positive change, and I trust in my ability to thrive.

Lux Shines

Bright soul, within the boundless cosmos, you are but the slightest flicker of light and yet your essence wields the potential to shape destinies across the world and beyond, even to distant realms in galaxies aeons away. You, both human and dragon, embody the paradox of existence. The chaos that resides within you drives you to establish order. Understand that control is an illusion. Embrace the turmoil of the universe, for chaotic moments are inevitable. Find serenity in accepting that which cannot be changed or undone. Know that few obstacles are insurmountable. While the world whirls around, refrain from squandering your energy on anxiety. Instead, act purposefully, lending your hands and thoughts to a higher calling. In this, you shall discover the path forward is not through control but transcendence.

Terra Speaks

In your world, little dragon, there are chaotic forces beyond your grasp to imagine. These forces may bring upheaval, akin to a tidal wave that can send you tumbling and have you feel you are drowning. The dread of such dis-order can blind you to the fact that chaos can also birth unforeseen rewards and opportunities. Understand that chaos is the harbinger of transformation and evolution. It challenges your adaptability and resilience.

My counsel to you, young one, is to maintain communication in moments of chaos. Find your own rhythm, and shed the superfluous. Create routines in your daily life, but also allow for spontaneity. Let go and embrace the moment. Sometimes, all you can do is take a deep breath and permit chaos to carry you along. Let it take you into uncharted seas. Change and growth are its ultimate purpose, and embracing it may uncover unexpected treasures hidden under the tempestuous seas of life.

Umbra Growls

Humans, you are chaotic creatures at the best of times. How do you accomplish anything within the mess that exists in your mind? You have forgotten how to be still. In doing so, your inner chaos manifests in your feelings, thoughts, and actions. It would not be a problem if your mind was not full of worry, doubt, and confusion. There is too much chaos. Your inner noisiness makes my own brain ache. Stop it! It is time for you to instil a little order within the chaos of your mind. It is time to become more disciplined. Stop leaving everything to the last minute and then wondering why all has become noise and confusion, making it hard to think. And for me to sleep.

Choice

Affirmation

In every moment, I hold the power of choice. With each decision, I shape my reality and define my path. I choose empowering thoughts and actions that align with my values. Faced with adversity, I choose resilience. In moments of doubt, I choose courage. With each choice, I honour my authenticity and embrace the journey of self-discovery. Today, I celebrate the freedom and responsibility that comes with my ability to choose.

Lux Shines

Bright soul, ponder the path you desire to follow on this cosmic journey. The Source of All grants you the gift of choice — a force that shapes your destiny. Each decision steers your existence, propelling you forward or anchoring you in the stillness of contemplation. Embrace the truth that you are the weaver of your fate, and your choices are the threads from which you create the tapestry that is your life. With profound choices, those that alter the very fabric of your being, consider the cosmic dance of *pro et contra* — the 'for and against'. Acknowledge the responsibility bound to your choices. Your decision will birth both blessings and tribulations. Freedom and responsibility are spun into every thread as inseparable cosmic partners. Recognise when you decide that no matter what you choose, there will be a toll, a cosmic tithe asked for your continued participation in the cosmic dance.

Terra Speaks

In the realm of mortal decisions, the power of choice has no straightforward path. Choices vary, presenting a spectrum of rewards and consequences. Some may offer outcomes that are collective triumphs, and prosperity graces all. Yet, in the complex nature of decisions, moments emerge where one path boasts meagre gains, and another harbours the weight of additional burdens and responsibilities. Life may confront you with choices devoid of joy, each outcome unwelcome. There will also be moments when two splendid opportunities beckon simultaneously, demanding a commitment to only one, with the other never arising again. Can you make the choice for one and not regret the loss of the other?

Let haste not lead you to make choices that offer irreversible outcomes. Also, be mindful of moral obligations that call upon you to choose for the greater good instead of personal gain. While limited or unwanted choices may be all you see, you must still choose and accept your part in the outcome. Mistakes are inevitable. Again, accept them and learn from them. The richness of choice will unveil itself when you explore beyond initial perceptions, and growth arises from embracing the lessons within each decision.

Umbra Growls

Foolish human. Do you seek refuge from the repercussions of your own folly? It is time to see that the path you shun may offer salvation. Stop looking for a magical panacea for the aftermath of countless unhealthy or unwise choices. Now, your power will be found in forging a virtuous path and following it with a disciplined determination. If financial ruin beckons, do not squander what you lack. If you seek forgiveness from others for the wounds their words and choice to leave have inflicted, then look at your role in the deeds that birthed the pain. Are you without fault? Blame dances on your tongue, a feeble attempt to evade accountability. Unpleasant as they may be, my words bear the weight of an undeniable truth. Take accountability, for in its crucible, the essence of your mettle is forged. The time has come to look upon and claim the tapestry your choices have woven.

Communicate

Affirmation

I communicate with clarity, compassion, and authenticity. My words carry the power to inspire, uplift, and connect. I listen attentively, seeking to understand before being understood. Through open dialogue, I foster deeper connections and cultivate meaningful relationships. Whether through spoken language or silent gestures, I convey my truth with integrity and empathy. Today, I embrace the art of communication as a catalyst for harmony, understanding, and positive change.

Lux Shines

Bright one, still yourself, and listen as the Divine whispers to your soul. The Source of All waits for your awareness. Seek not only with mortal ears, but with your spirit. In the quiet spaces, hear the subtle hum of universal truths, and let the cosmic currents guide you. Understand that communication with the Divine transcends words. It's an exchange of energies, a dance of vibrations. Open your heart to the cosmic resonance, and you shall find communion with the ineffable. Hear the songs of distant stars with their subtle cadence. The ancient wisdom of the cosmos unfolds. Trust the sacred dialogue, for you are a part of the cosmic conversation, and in the stillness, the universe reveals its secrets.

Terra Speaks

Heed me, little dragon. The art of communication is not a mystical riddle, so refrain from offering riddles or embellished tales. Eye contact is the bridge between souls, so meet the gaze of those you speak with so they can see your truth. I know this is a challenging task for some, but do your best because sometimes the eyes have to be seen for the words spoken to be heard.

Honesty is the key to understanding. Choose your words with care, for they carry weight beyond measure. Honesty without kindness is an often-unnecessary act of born of a damaged ego. Speak intending to support, nurture, and heal. Words should not be used to harm or disempower without good or just reason.

Understand that sometimes silence is required. Sometimes, words must give way to the quiet strength of understanding. Learn to feel the rhythm of reciprocity. Conversations are a dance for two or more, not a solo act.

Finally, acknowledge the power of empathy, for it is a force that creates lasting connections.

Umbra Growls

In this earthly realm, effective communication is a skill forged in sincerity, tempered with patience, and honed through genuine connection. Let your words create connections instead of breaking them.

Put your judgement and expectations to the side. Be

present in every conversation, not just physically but with your full attention. Listen with your mind and heart open as well as your ears.

When there is a misunderstanding, human, cast aside the arrogance of ego, admit fault when needed and be respectful but firm when it is not. Remember, a conversation is a sharing of knowledge or information, not a battle of wills or dominance. Your words have power. There is no need to turn your words into weapons that inflict permanent harm. Say what is necessary and leave what's not unsaid. It isn't your place to tell others how to be just because you believe you know better. You do not.

Conflict

Affirmation

In moments of conflict, I see opportunities for growth and understanding. I approach disagreements with an open mind and a compassionate spirit. Through active listening and respectful dialogue, I seek common ground and mutual respect. Conflict can be a pathway to deeper connections and strengthened relationships. With patience and empathy, I navigate conflicts with grace and integrity.

Lux Shines

Where humans tread, conflict emerges, inevitable as the stars' dance. Just as two galaxies can crash together in the vastness of the universe, clashes will arise from disparate minds colliding in the realm of individuality. No mandate binds you to embrace another's beliefs, yet it is necessary to recognise their sacred right to existence and joy. Respecting diverse paths demands no communion, while understanding births harmony. Should no harm ripple outward from their choices, treat them with the same grace you hope others will show you. Quell the dragon's fire of arrogance, bright soul, and soar from needless strife. Embrace the mantra of live and let live. Preserve your radiant warrior essence for battles against injustice or shielding the vulnerable. In those moments, be valiant and stand unwavering, a fierce cosmic champion of justice and truth.

Terra Speaks

Little dragon, conflicts will occur in even the most loving relationship, sparking heated exchanges and bitter words. Do not shy away from the discord nor cloak it in silence. Avoid the pitfalls of punishment or submission. Instead, confront the issue, preventing its insidious roots from poisoning your bond. Silence is the friend of an unresolved argument and can erode love and trust. Speak, little dragon. Share your heart's sorrows and fears with respect but without accusations and condemnation. Then, listen to their own heart's sorrows and fears. Seek compromise but also demand reciprocity in care. Let your voice be a gentle breeze, dispersing the storm clouds of conflict, nurturing the fertile ground where understanding may thrive, even when that understanding reveals the way forward to be one where you agree to disagree.

Umbra Growls

Human, why do you persist in your obstinate rebellion, challenging authority with impiety unchecked? Stubbornness, defiance, outrage — your intent merely to disturb those you perceive to be against or obstructing you. Rebellion has its place and time, but your contrary nature seems to serve only chaos. Why this relentless attack, this delight in verbal fisticuffs? Find an outlet for that aggression ... a punching bag, maybe? Cease the conflict, abandon the drama, and halt your demolition of others' peace of mind. Your insatiable thirst for strife unveils a reservoir of buried anger and turmoil. Seek an impartial confidant to illuminate the shadows within. The time has come to confront the source of your internal anger before it does irreparable harm to your relationships.

Connection

Affirmation

I am woven into the fabric of universal connection, bound by threads of love, empathy, and understanding. In every interaction, I nurture meaningful bonds that transcend barriers. With an open heart, I embrace the beauty of shared experiences and mutual respect. Through connection, I find strength, joy, and purpose. Today, I celebrate the richness of human connection, knowing that together, we create a tapestry of belonging and unity.

Lux Shines

In the cosmic tapestry of existence, visible and unseen threads weave together, forming a seamless connection. Understand, mortal, that at your essence, you are pure energy emanating from the boundless Source of All. You are not separate, you are a harmonious note in the symphony of creation. Born of the Divine, you possess inherent divinity. Your thoughts, feelings, and beliefs resonate not only within your perception, but reverberate throughout the cosmos to touch all and everything. Embrace the profound truth, bright soul, and allow your beauty and goodness to shine. You wield the power to shape reality, for you are a reflection of the cosmic dance. Let your compassionate heart lead, for in doing so, you embody the transformative change you seek in the world around you. Feel the dragon spirit within rising to celestial heights, where it shall dance as one with and in the celestial expanse.

Terra Speaks

Heed an ancient truth: your actions ripple through the interconnected threads of life. Little dragon, I share wisdom carried by the winds of time with you. When you fell a tree, you take its breath from the world. That breath sustains you. When you plant a field over and over again using pesticides and poisons, you eventually kill the soil in which your food grows. You starve the roots that sustain you. The soil contains life that connects everything, and it withers under the weight of your abuse and neglect. The barrens will replace life if humanity cannot acknowledge and cherish its connection with the earth. Recognise the price of actions, even those born of unknowing. In harming others, you harm yourself as Gaia's heartbeat echoes in your own.

Umbra Growls

What is it you humans say? Karma is a bitch? Well, that's a truth you find funny whilst you watch as others are slapped on the head for the wrong they have done. You stop laughing when karma catches up with you for being judgemental. So many believe karma will greet you in your next life, but what if this is the only one? Human, I'm not inclined to give you spoilers. I will offer this: karma is an energetic exchange, and because we are all energy and connected, the seeds of your karma will be sown instantaneously. Check your energy. Are you looking for trouble? Spoiling for a fight? Have less than pure intentions? Feel like laughing at another's distress? Know you will be met with what you project. If you cannot move through life with compassion in your heart and a kind word for everyone, then at least be prepared to be met with an energy that mirrors your own. And remember that mud sticks. You might believe you've gotten away with something, but your actions mark your energy for good or ill. Your karma is earned instantly, but she can also be patient and catch up with you when you least expect it.

CREATE

AFFIRMATION

I am a vessel of boundless creativity, shaping worlds with my imagination and passion, and breathing life into my dreams with each brushstroke, keystroke, or heartfelt gesture. I trust in the power of my ideas and the beauty of my vision. In every act of creation, I honour my unique voice and express my truth. Today, I embrace the joy of bringing something new into existence, knowing that within me lies endless potential.

LUX SHINES

Bright soul, look up into the universe and behold the wonder of creation woven by the threads of divine essence. I, one of the very first souls to be born of the Void, have witnessed the birth of existence, where each particle of energy and atom has danced in harmony according to the cosmic design. Understand that creation is not merely a singular act, but an ongoing manifestation of divine intention. Marvel at the beauty of creation and find comfort knowing that you, too, are a part of this grand and cosmic design. You are more than just matter. You matter. Embrace your role with pure intent and purpose. In doing so, you honour your Divine Creator.

Terra Speaks

Listen close, little dragon. Heed the wisdom of the earth — creativity is not a distant spark bestowed upon the chosen few. It's a fire burning within each and every soul. To nurture this flame, immerse yourself in the world around you. Observe, absorb, and allow your experiences to fuel your imagination. Do not fear failure, for it is the raw material from which great works are sculpted. Just remember to be disciplined in your craft, for even the wildest ideas require structure to flourish. Be open to collaboration with fellow artisans. Together, you'll forge ideas stronger than any lone endeavour. Like the roots of ancient trees, let your creativity dig deep, anchoring you amidst life's storms. And when doubt creeps in, remember — within you lies the power to not only shape the world around you but also to create worlds.

Umbra Growls

Human, one of the harshest truths you shall learn is this — creation and destruction are twin forces intertwined in the cosmic dance of existence. To create is to destroy, for every birth heralds the end of what once was. Embrace this duality, for it is the essence of life itself. Do not condemn or fear destruction. Instead, wield it as a tool for transformation. Embrace the small deaths life offers. Mourn, yes, but understand that they hold the power to birth new beginnings from the ashes of the old. Accept that in every act of creation, there lies the seed of destruction, and in every act of destruction, there lies the spark of creation. It is up to you to forge your destiny amidst the chaos of both.

Dance

Affirmation

In the rhythm of life, I find my dance — a sacred expression of joy, freedom, and self-discovery. With every step, I surrender to the music of my soul, letting it guide me with grace and passion. In the fluidity of movement, I release inhibitions and embrace authenticity. Dance is my language, speaking volumes of love, resilience, and vitality. Today, I celebrate the beauty of dance as a pathway to liberation and inner harmony.

Lux Shines

Bright soul, the universe is in constant motion, dancing an eternal dance. From galaxies swirling to your own heartbeat, all is in motion. Nothing is still. Everything vibrates. Close your eyes. Feel the pulse of existence, guiding the cosmos along its destined course. Feel it and embrace its rhythm in a life where challenges and opportunities dance as one. Trust. Harmonise your soul with the universe's heartbeat and find everything you need to stay strong amidst turmoil. Do not resist and increase your suffering. Give yourself over to the Divine. Dance your dance with sure feet, knowing that in the darkest night there will be stars to illuminate your path forward.

Terra Speaks

Little dragon, movement is a key value of life, essential for body and soul. You are not meant to be still. Engage in regular exercise, for it strengthens your form and clears the mind. But do not constrain yourself to unenjoyable forms of movement. Why not embrace the joy of dancing? Let your body sway to the earth's rhythm, connecting with its primal energy. Dance not for perfection but for the sheer delight of movement. Explore different styles, from a forest creature's wild leaps to a river's graceful flow. Find what moves your spirit and dance with abandon. It matters not how skilled or how you move. Just move with purpose and joy. Heed the call of the earth's rhythm and dance like flames in the night, fierce and free.

Umbra Growls

Hear me, human, and heed my words. Your stillness breeds decay that drains both body and spirit of vitality. By ignoring your body's need for movement, you court your end. You allow your body to waste and disease to consume your essence. Life dances around you, and yet you take no part, preferring to cling to inertia. Get up. Join in. Embrace the challenge of movement. Fear not the unfamiliar steps — take one step at a time toward growth and strength. It is time to move with intent and make your body, mind, and spirit strong or face the consequences of your neglect.

Dichotomy

Affirmation

In the dance of opposites, I discover unity — a harmonious blend of light and shadow, strength and vulnerability. Embracing the dichotomy within, I find balance and wholeness. In darkness, I uncover hidden truths. In light, I see boundless potential. Each contradiction enriches my journey, offering lessons of resilience and growth. Today, I honour the beauty of dichotomy, knowing that within its paradox lies the essence of my humanity and the depth of my soul.

Lux Shines

In the vast expanse of existence, dichotomies weave their threads, guiding the dance of creation. Yet, bright soul, you must beware of the allure of oversimplification, for reality transcends mere binaries. Embrace the nuance, for within the spectrum lies the truth. Creation and destruction, order and chaos, life and death, and light and dark are all aspects of the same whole. Seek not to confine the universe within narrow bounds, but instead, open your mind to its boundless complexity. Let not the need to categorise and simplify blind you to the true beauty and majesty of the tapestry that unites and binds all things. Embrace the infinite possibilities of existence and soar among the stars with eyes wide open to the wonders of the cosmos.

Terra Speaks

Little dragon, within the realms of this earthly plane, dichotomies influence all aspects of life — predator and prey, light and darkness, growth and decay. However, humanity is not confined to one side or the other. Instead, it dances between extremes. Like the herbivore turned hunter, you possess the capacity for both gentleness and ferocity. You are both a producer and a consumer of life. That said, you cannot live without ending life. You can do great good, but your very existence comes at the cost of other living things. You are death, but also a catalyst of growth and an agent of change because you can change your mind, choose your path, and determine how light or heavy your step is upon this earth. You live in a reality that is shaped by day and night, but you are not bound by it. Somewhere in between the dichotomous extremes is a place of harmonious accord. Seek it, for therein lies strength and wisdom.

Umbra Growls

Human, your fixation on dichotomous thinking is a weakness. Life isn't merely black or white, there's a vast spectrum in between. Avoid labelling individuals and situations as solely right or wrong, good or bad. We all possess complexities beyond our sometimes-shallow judgements. It is time for you to understand that there are circumstances when two opposing forces can both have just cause to act as an aggressor, and times when the behaviour of both is founded on a desire to gain control and nothing more. Yes, there are times when one is in the right, and the other is in the wrong. One attacks unjustly, without good reason, but even in those situations, there is often something more going on beneath the surface. There is always a reason. Sometimes we are innocent casualties of a secondary situation. Nothing is ever just black and white. Still, when something feels wrong, there will come a time when you will be forced to do what's right for you.

Direction

Affirmation

I am the captain of my ship, steering towards my chosen horizon with clarity and purpose. With each decision, I chart a course that aligns with my dreams and values. Even amidst uncertainty, I trust my inner compass to guide me towards fulfilment and success. I embrace each turn, knowing that every change in direction brings new opportunities for growth and discovery. Today, I navigate my path with confidence, courage, and conviction.

Lux Shines

Bright soul, within the boundless expanse of the heavens above, there exists a celestial current. Align your body, mind, and spirit with this divine flow. It will take you to where you are meant to be. Trust that you have a divine purpose and will be taken in the direction you need to go, with every choice and action in accord with the heartbeat of the universe. Rather than seeking to control every outcome, have faith and surrender to the natural flow of an unfolding destiny. Remember, you are made of stardust. You are intimately connected, an integral part of the universe. It's time to look to the heavens and step into a starlit stream of consciousness.

Terra Speaks

Having a direction in life is akin to wielding a compass in a maze — it provides clarity and purpose in moments when there are no visible landmarks to guide you. Define your goals, little dragon, for they serve as beacons guiding your journey through the labyrinth. With direction, decisions become clearer and obstacles are more manageable. Embrace your ambitions, for they fuel your determination and drive. But remember, flexibility is key. Adjust your course as the terrain shifts. Stay steadfast in pursuit of your dreams, and you shall navigate life's twists and turns with greater ease.

Umbra Growls

Listen closely, human, to the truth hidden within your shadow. Without purpose, you drift through life without direction, squandering a precious gift. I know you question your reason for being and purpose, but your purpose is to live and to fill your life with meaning. It is time to set a goal and let it become your guiding light. It does not have to be a huge goal. The greater the goal, the greater the risk of failure, and right now, your confidence needs a few wins. Set small, achievable goals fuelled by need, interest, and curiosity. Fear not the unknown or what others will say. This is your life to live and your path to walk. Choose a direction and take those first steps. You might stumble, but we are here, watching over you. We will not let you fall.

Fears

Affirmation

Fear is a gateway to courage. In its presence, I discover my inner strength, resilience, and potential. I face my fears with open arms, knowing they hold the key to growth and transformation. With each step forward, I embrace discomfort and uncertainty, knowing they lead to profound self-discovery. Fear is not my enemy but my ally, propelling me towards greatness. Today, I rise above my fears, embodying courage, determination, and unwavering faith in myself.

Lux Shines

Bright soul, heed this divine truth. Your fears are not your foe, but instead a compass guiding your journey. Embrace their whispers not with trembling, but with the recognition and certainty of your own strength. Within their shadowy depths, dormant power waits for you to draw upon it. Let your fears be the forge of your resilience and the crucible of your growth. Do not give in to whispers that speak of restriction and limitation. Instead, harness the power within you to soar higher and overcome all doubts. Remember always your divinity and transcend the suffocating grasp of your fears. Acknowledge them, understand that you are allowed to be afraid, but then embrace your fears and watch as they transmute into the force propelling you towards your destiny.

Terra Speaks

Fear, little dragon, is a force as ancient as the mountains, but many fail to understand that its power lies in the present moment. Face your fears head on. When you allow the fear of an unknown future to cast a shadow over your present, it dims the light of your potential. Ground yourself in the here and now, like roots anchoring a mighty tree. Take decisive action, for it is in that moment your fears lose their grip. Trust in your innate resilience, like the earth enduring the fiercest storms. Even if your fears are realised, you will recover, continue to grow and even thrive. Seize each moment as an opportunity to shape your future, for it is in the present that your future takes form.

Umbra Growls

Human, why do you constantly strive to be fearless? Why do you judge those who voice their fears and label them as negative? It is foolish to believe that you can be, or should be, without fear. Not to mention, exhausting. Fear is as vital as the air you breathe. Fear sharpens instincts, ignites caution, and fuels growth. If you feel it, acknowledge its presence. Don't dismiss it, but also do not allow it to shackle your spirit. Instead, wield it as a tool for discernment. Wisdom is knowing there is a difference between rational caution and irrational dread. Understand that discomfort is an opportunity to progress, for beyond its threshold lies transformation. But beware the poison of excessive fear, for it paralyses action and stifles potential. Cultivate a balanced relationship with fear by allowing it to guide but not dominate. It is not the absence of fear that defines strength, but the mastery of it.

Flow

Affirmation

In the gentle embrace of flow, I surrender to the rhythm of life. Like a river carving its path, I move effortlessly with the currents of change. In flow, I find harmony, creativity, and inner peace. I release resistance and embrace acceptance, trusting in the wisdom of the universe. Today, I allow myself to be carried by the flow, knowing that within its embrace, I find serenity, purpose, and boundless possibilities.

Lux Shines

In the dance of existence, there is a sublime state that transcends the confines of time. When you find yourself immersed in the flow of life, time loses its grip, and you become one with the infinite heartbeat of the universe. Bright soul, embrace these moments of pure harmony and alignment, for they are a blessing from the Divine. Like the celestial dragon that traverses the cosmos without constraint, allow yourself to be flowing and free, unburdened by the limitations of time and space. In these moments, you discover that happiness can be found in surrender.

Terra Speaks

The river teaches a timeless lesson — to go with the flow. Just as the river adapts to the twists and turns of the land, so too must you adjust to life's ever-changing currents. Be like water, flowing and fluid, and trust in its wisdom, for it follows the path of least resistance. Little dragon, when faced with obstacles, flow around them like water does a rock rather than fighting against the current. Remember, the river may meander but always finds its way to the sea. So too, will you find your path if you surrender to the natural flow of life, guided by the ancient wisdom of the river.

Umbra Growls

Listen closely, human. Surrendering to the whims of others will only lead to your demise. Going with the flow to appease others is an exercise in futility akin to choosing to swim in a mud puddle. Navigate your own course. Do not be swept away by the demands and expectations of others. Stand firm in your convictions, even if it means facing turbulent waters alone. Remember, true respect is earned by staying true to yourself, not by following a course another has set for you. Be aware that there are times when going with the flow does not signify ease. Sometimes, it means surviving the rapids until you are carried to peaceful waters.

Focus

Affirmation

In this moment, I harness the power of my mind. Like a laser beam, I channel my energy towards my goals with unwavering determination. Distractions fade away as I immerse myself in the present moment. With clarity and intent, I take purposeful steps towards my dreams. Today, I am focused, knowing this is the key to unlocking my potential and achieving greatness.

Lux Shines

Within you resides a boundless wellspring of energy, a divine spark connecting you with the universe. Bright soul, I urge you to channel this energy wisely. Focus your thoughts on love, for it is the purest force in existence. Allow it to be your primary source of motivation, the force that guides your every action. Embrace love in this moment, for love is the source of all miracles. With every breath, you shape your reality. Focus your energy, set your intention, let your heart be your compass, and let love be your guiding star.

Terra Speaks

I commend you for your pursuit of passion and purpose, little dragon. To harness your special interests, focus on consistency and commitment. Dive deep into your chosen pursuits, immersing yourself in their intricacies. Set specific goals to keep your journey on track, but remain flexible in your approach. Embrace challenges as opportunities for growth, for they fortify your resolve. Surround yourself with like-minded individuals who inspire and support you. These people should respect your commitment and help you to stay focused instead of offering distractions. Remember, success is not measured by speed but by perseverance. So, cultivate patience and resilience to keep your passion ignited. Let your enthusiasm and determination fuel your focus.

Umbra Growls

Listen up, little human. I may breathe fire, but I'm not here to roast marshmallows. You're flitting around like a butterfly in a flower field, focusing on everything except what truly matters. Stop chasing every shiny distraction! It's time to stop dividing your focus. Identify what you must do and lock onto it like a predator tracking its prey. Sure, there are a thousand paths you could take, but they lead you away from your goals, not to them. Don't squander your energy on fruitless endeavours. Focus, discipline, and determination are your allies. I know it can be difficult. I know you humans sometimes struggle with inner critics who belittle or offer distractions to help you sabotage your goal. You need to ignore them. Heed my words or face the consequences — because there will be consequences if you do not focus your energy on completing the tasks that need to be done now, not later.

Forewarning

Affirmation

Forewarning is my ally, guiding me with foresight and intuition. I heed its gentle whispers, preparing myself for the journey ahead. With awareness and readiness, I face challenges with grace and resilience. Forewarning illuminates hidden paths, empowering me to make informed decisions. Today, I embrace its wisdom, knowing that in its guidance lies the power to overcome obstacles and thrive in every circumstance.

Lux Shines

Bright soul, it is time for you to shine your brightest. You are a beacon of hope and authenticity to those who will need your light in times ahead. Be the best example of humanity you can be for a dragon. Be loving. Be empathetic. Be compassionate. Be generous. Be kind. Let your wings be shelter for those in need. Despite whatever challenge you may face, meet it with equanimity. Meet the wave that comes with a peaceful heart. You have been forewarned, so now you can prepare. To step into this higher purpose, you must be honest with yourself. You must divest yourself of the beliefs that would have you judging others and thinking them less. Raise others up by showing them they too have dragon wings and a dragon's spirit.

Terra Speaks

Red sky at night, sailors' delight.
Red sky in morning, sailors' take warning.
When the clouds look like black smoke, a wise man puts on his cloak.

Little dragon, sometimes the natural world will offer a forewarning. Bad weather is not an absolute, but noting the conditions gives you the opportunity to plan for a bad-weather outcome. It is also important to note 'conditions' in other areas of your life. There will be times when others offer information that gives you advance notice of a potential situation that needs to be planned for — pay attention! For example, you might mention that you want to go back to school. A friend might tell you that you need to be able to commit to at least 20 hours of study a week for the course that interests you. You have full-time employment and a family to look after. What will you need to do to free up this time? Learn everything you can—the good, the bad, and the unanticipated—before you make a commitment to any circumstance that you might not keep because the unanticipated aspects made it impossible.

Umbra Growls

While it is best not to fall into a habit of gossiping, sometimes it pays to listen to rumours and read the bad reviews. They often give insight as to a person's or organisation's reputation and how they treat others. Sometimes, the criticism and complaints have foundation. Do you believe someone to be a good person? If they are, then why are there so many dead and wounded in their wake? Even a good person cannot help but hurt others now and again, but if there has been more than one, and they've all been harmed in similar ways ...? Don't be foolish, human. Yes, we can all have very different experiences when it comes to people, but it pays to be cautious if an individual or organisation has done wrong to others. If they have done wrong to more than one, then it might be in your best interests to be careful.

Fulfilment

Affirmation

In pursuing fulfilment, I embrace the journey with gratitude and purpose. Each moment and experience bring me closer to my highest potential. I find fulfilment in the growth and joy I experience along the way. With an open heart and a determined spirit, I create a life rich in meaning and abundance. Today, I celebrate my blessings, knowing I am exactly where I need to be.

Lux Shines

Bright soul, understand that fulfilment is a deeply personal, subjective, and ultimately, divine experience. It is about finding satisfaction, contentment, and purpose in life. More than simple happiness or pleasure, it involves a feeling, a profound sense of purpose and meaning in one's actions, relationships, and contributions to the world. By living authentically and embracing the challenges and joys that you experience will can help you to find a sense of wholeness and satisfaction in your journey. It's a dynamic state that evolves as you grow and change throughout your life. Ultimately, it's about feeling complete and aligned with your values, goals, and aspirations. Being and feeling as one with all and everything.

Terra Speaks

Your unique way of experiencing the world is a gift, little dragon. To find fulfilment, embrace your strengths and passions, knowing they are the keys to unlocking your true potential. Seek environments and activities that align with your interests and provide opportunities for growth. Practise self-care and self-acceptance, honouring your needs and boundaries. Surround yourself with supportive people who appreciate and celebrate your individuality. Remember, fulfilment is not a destination but a journey of self-discovery and growth. Celebrate your victories, no matter how small, and be patient with yourself during challenges. Trust in your inner wisdom and resilience. Embrace your identity with confidence, allowing it to be a source of strength and empowerment on your path to fulfilment.

Umbra Growls

It's time to break free from the self-imposed barriers of self-criticism and dissatisfaction that are holding you back from fulfilling your potential and from feeling fulfilled. Stop striving for perfection. It's nothing but an illusion. Instead, recognise and embrace your unique strengths and imperfections as part of what makes you extraordinary. Challenge negative self-talk by practising self-compassion and gratitude. And, human, stop wasting your time comparing yourself to others; instead, focus on your own individual growth and aspirations, and be realistic in how you approach them. You are deserving of love and acceptance just as you are. By cultivating self-kindness and embracing your authentic self, you can break free from the shackles of self-criticism and dissatisfaction, paving the way to true fulfilment.

Give and Receive

Affirmation
In the dance of giving and receiving, I find balance and abundance. I give freely from my heart, knowing that generosity nourishes the soul. In receiving, I embrace humility and gratitude, allowing love and kindness to flow into my life. Each act of giving creates ripples of joy and connection, enriching the life of both the giver and the receiver. Today, I honour the beautiful exchange of giving and receiving, knowing it fills my life with meaning and purpose.

Lux Shines
Bright soul, in this infinite dance of life, giving and receiving are sacred exchanges that flow in perfect harmony with the universe. They are like the gentle ebb and flow of the tides, always intertwined in the interconnected fabric of our existence. You possess the incredible ability to give from the boundless wellspring of love that lives within you. Every kind word, every helping hand, and every attentive ear you offer to others sends ripples of compassion throughout the world, enriching the lives of all you touch. Similarly, it's essential to embrace

the divine gift of receiving. Allow yourself to be open to the love, support, and kindness of others. This act of vulnerability not only connects you to your fellow humans but also affirms your inherent worthiness to receive the boundless blessings of the universe. Remember to cherish the sacred balance of giving and receiving, for it's in this reciprocity that the essence of our shared humanity lies.

Terra Speaks

Little dragon, in the grand dance of life, our connection to the environment and Earth is profound and intricate. Your connection to the world around you allows you to give and receive in ways that even you may not fully comprehend. Embrace the gifts you bring to this symbiotic exchange. Whether it's through appreciating natural beauty, nurturing plants and creating natural spaces for wildlife, minimising your impact upon the earth, or advocating for conservation, your contributions matter. Remember, Mother Earth offers boundless gifts in return — solace, inspiration, sustenance, shelter, and life. Find solace and strength in this relationship. Your connection to the planet is not just about giving or receiving — it's about fostering a harmonious relationship that nourishes both you and the world around you.

Umbra Growls

Navigating relationships and projects can be tough, human, especially when your innate desire to please others collides with the reality of unequal give-and-take. It's important to recognise the risks of overextending yourself. Continuously prioritising others' needs over your own can lead to burnout, resentment, and an imbalance in relationships and projects. Remember, your worth is not defined by how much you give or accomplish. Set boundaries, communicate your needs clearly, and prioritise self-care. Surround yourself with those who value and reciprocate your efforts. Your contributions are valuable, and you deserve to be treated fairly. It's essential to maintain a healthy balance of giving and receiving in all things. Don't be afraid to speak up for yourself and take charge of your own wellbeing.

Gratitude

Affirmation

Gratitude is my guiding light, illuminating the blessings that surround me. In every moment, I embrace abundance. In gratitude, I find joy, peace, and profound connection. I cultivate thankfulness for both the big and small gifts of life, knowing that appreciation magnifies my bounty. Today, I live in gratitude, allowing its transformative power to uplift my spirit and enrich my journey.

Lux Shines
Gratitude is like a shining beacon of hope that can help you navigate the ups and downs of life. It's a thread that weaves its way through the fabric of your existence, connecting you to the universe. When you express gratitude, you open yourself up to the transformative power of positivity and connection. Whether you share your gratitude with others through words or actions, or simply reflect on all that you have to be thankful for, you invite warmth and light into your life. In moments of both joy and struggle, gratitude can serve as a reminder that there is always something to be grateful for, even amidst the challenges you face. Bright soul, by embracing gratitude as a divine gift, you can find nourishment for your souls and discover the richness of life's experiences.

Terra Speaks
Little dragon, expressing gratitude is a powerful practice that can bring joy and positivity into your life. Why not try creating a gratitude journal filled with sensory experiences or crafting art pieces that capture moments of appreciation? You could also incorporate gratitude practices into your daily routine, like morning stretches or bedtime reflections, to make it a habit. Have you considered creating a gratitude collage with textures and colours that resonate with you? Gratitude has no limits, so let your imagination run wild and express your gratitude in ways that feel authentic and meaningful to you.

Umbra Growls

You humans tend to be blind to the abundance surrounding you, especially when fear, distress, or one of life's many challenges cloud your perception. However, failing to recognise this abundance can lead to a sense of ingratitude, obscuring the opportunities awaiting discovery. It's important to remember that within every obstacle lies a hidden opportunity, and within every challenge is a lesson waiting to be learned. To cultivate gratitude, open your eyes to the richness of life's offerings, no matter how small they might seem. Shift your perspective. Doing so may give you the key to uncovering opportunities that you may have overlooked. Take a moment to pause, breathe, and appreciate the abundance within and around you. Gratitude transforms scarcity into abundance, unlocking the doors to endless possibilities.

Guide

Affirmation

As I journey forward, I trust in the wisdom of my inner guide. With every step, I listen to its gentle whispers, leading me towards my highest path. In times of uncertainty, it offers clarity and reassurance. I embrace its guidance with gratitude, knowing it lights the way to my true purpose. Today, I surrender to the loving direction of my inner guide, confident in its ability to navigate me towards fulfilment and growth.

Lux Shines

Life can be puzzling and full of uncertainties, bright soul. In such times, divine guidance can serve as a steadfast beacon, illuminating your path and providing solace, clarity, and direction. No matter what obstacles you face, connecting with the Divine can align you with universal wisdom and unconditional love. Trust in your intuition and the signs and synchronicities that will appear in your life, for divine guidance offers a sanctuary amidst life's storms and a gentle hand guiding you towards your true purpose and highest potential. Embrace this sacred connection, for within it lies the answers to life's deepest questions and the comfort of knowing you are never alone on this journey.

Terra Speaks

Little dragon, I want to remind you that your journey is a source of inspiration for others who are going through similar struggles. You have the power to guide them with empathy and kindness by sharing your experiences and knowledge. Your unique perspective can offer valuable insights and hope to those seeking guidance. Remember to approach your role as a guide with a humble and compassionate heart, and let others find their own way to be themselves. By sharing your light and passion, you can bring hope and positive change to the lives of those around you. Always remember that you are not alone, and that your journey can inspire others to find their own strength and resilience.

Umbra Growls

It's important to remember that believing one knows what's best for others can lead to a dangerous path of arrogance and control. This, human, is me cautioning you against telling others what to do or how to live their lives. Every individual's journey is unique and shaped by personal experiences and aspirations. Assuming authority over others' choices disregards their autonomy and the diversity of perspectives. It fosters resentment, stifles growth, and erodes trust within relationships. True empowerment comes from honouring each person's autonomy and respecting their right to make decisions aligned with their values and aspirations. Guide, yes, but do so by embracing humility, empathy, and understanding.

Hope

Affirmation

In the depths of uncertainty, hope is my beacon of light. It fuels my spirit with courage and resilience. With each breath, I nurture the flame of hope, believing in the promise of brighter days ahead. In hope, I find the strength to persevere through challenges and embrace the unknown with optimism. Today, I hold on to hope as my guiding force, knowing it leads me towards a future filled with possibility and joy.

Lux Shines

Bright soul, I understand that life can be full of challenges. However, I want you to know that you possess a beautiful light and an unwavering spirit of resilience and possibility. You have the power of hope within you, which can light up even the darkest of paths. I encourage you to hold on to this hope tightly and let it guide you through life's ever-changing landscape. Remember that amidst uncertainty and adversity, hope is the beacon that leads you towards brighter tomorrows. Nurture it, cherish it, and let it be your guiding star. With hope as your compass, there are no limits to what you can achieve. Keep shining brightly and know that hope is the key to unlocking the extraordinary within you.

Terra Speaks

Amidst the looming environmental crisis, maintaining hope is not just essential, little dragon — it's the greatest catalyst for change. Hope fuels resilience, motivating humanity to take collective action and mitigate the impacts of climate change, extinction events, deforestation, and pollution. It inspires innovation, driving humanity to develop sustainable solutions and advocate for policy reforms. Despite daunting challenges, hope empowers you to envision a future where humanity and nature thrive in harmony. By remaining hopeful, you can become agents of positive change, contributing to a more sustainable and equitable world for future generations. Do not give up on hope. Let it be your guiding light and inspire you to act towards creating a brighter, more resilient future. With unwavering hope and collective action, humanity can navigate the environmental crisis and build a more sustainable tomorrow.

Umbra Growls

Human, I may be a creature of shadow, I may be blunt, but I am not heartless. I have felt the shadow of hopelessness that suffocates the spirit and makes one a prisoner. I sense it has you in its grip. I know you feel lost. I know how hopelessness drains your energy, destroys your motivation, and erodes your resilience. Consumed by hopelessness, you have surrendered your power to make a choice and to effect change. You have resigned yourself to a bleak existence devoid of possibility. Blind to opportunities, hopelessness has bred despair and apathy. It is a vicious cycle that perpetuates suffering and stagnation. But, I see you, human. I am here to ask you not to give up. This dragon gifts you with an eternal spark of hope. Let it transform you. Let it give you the strength to overcome adversity and find your way home.

Intimacy

Affirmation

In the sacred space of intimacy, I lower my walls and remove my masks. With trust as my foundation, I share vulnerabilities, weaving bonds of deep connection and understanding. Intimacy is the essence of love, where hearts intertwine and souls merge in profound union. Today, I embrace intimacy as a gift, cherishing connection, nurturing shared bonds with tenderness, honesty, and unwavering presence.

Lux Shines

Life is a beautiful gift that we are all blessed with. And it can become even more beautiful if we allow ourselves to form a deeper and more intimate connection with the Divine. Sometimes, life can be overwhelming and we may feel lost. But you need to trust that you are not alone and that you have a purpose. You are meant to be the magical and unique person you are. The Divine loves and cherishes you for who you are. Bright soul, you deserve to feel at peace and confident. It is time for you to explore and follow a path that will increase your understanding of the energy that surrounds you and flows within you, and how your thoughts and beliefs influence it. Embrace the Divine in all that you do, in body, mind, and spirit. Let the Divine's love flow through you.

Terra Speaks

Developing emotional intimacy is the foundation of a meaningful relationship that nourishes trust, comprehension, and connection, little dragon. To establish and maintain it, it's crucial to prioritise kind and honest communication, and share your emotions, thoughts, and vulnerabilities with your partner. It's important to listen actively and acknowledge their feelings, which will promote mutual respect and empathy. Make an effort to create quality time together, taking part in activities that strengthen your bond and form shared memories. It's essential to foster a supportive and safe environment where both partners can express themselves without fear of criticism. Show affection and appreciation, and express love and gratitude often. Finally, prioritise the growth and evolution of your relationship, knowing that emotional intimacy requires continuous effort, patience, and dedication from both partners. By working on emotional intimacy, you will create an enduring and satisfying relationship.

Umbra Growls

Human, it's time to take accountability for the disharmony within your relationship. When one partner seeks emotional and physical intimacy while being unable to reciprocate, it creates an imbalanced dynamic that can lead to resentment, disappointment, and heartbreak. This mismatch in emotional and physical availability undermines trust and erodes the foundation of the relationship, hindering its growth and longevity. Why are you creating distance when you want closeness? It's crucial to address any barriers that prevent you from giving and receiving intimacy. Communicate openly, be empathetic, and be willing to work through this challenge together. It is what you need in order to heal and maintain your relationship. Remember, true intimacy thrives on mutual understanding, vulnerability, and reciprocity. So, it's time to take responsibility and work towards building a relationship where both partners feel safe, seen, heard, fulfilled, and valued.

Journey

Affirmation

My journey is a tapestry of growth woven with threads of resilience, discovery, and transformation. Each step forward is a testament to my courage and determination. Along the way, I embrace the lessons of the past, and eagerly anticipate the blessings of the future. With an open heart and a steadfast spirit, I navigate life's twists and turns, knowing that every experience enriches my soul and propels me towards my highest purpose.

Lux Shines

In the kaleidoscope of existence, our souls embark on a journey as diverse and intricate as the human mind. Embracing divergent thinking enriches this odyssey, infusing it with boundless creativity, resilience, and insight. Our unique perspectives and experiences shape our path, weaving a tapestry of united diversity. Create a mind that embraces ideas and beliefs that offer a range of perspectives, while illuminating hidden truths and expanding your understanding of the universe. Embrace the beauty of your soul's journey. Celebrate the richness this life brings to your collective human experience.

Navigate this journey with compassion, curiosity, and reverence, honouring the myriad ways the human mind explores, perceives, and creates. By embracing diversity, bright soul, we unlock the potential for profound growth, connection, and the transformation of your soul.

Terra Speaks

Little dragon, your experiences in life play a significant role in shaping your thoughts and actions. Each experience—whether good or bad—moulds you into the individual you are today. By learning from these experiences, you develop resilience and empathy that, in turn, help you overcome future challenges with confidence and grace. By reflecting on these experiences, you also gain wisdom and insight that guide you through future situations. Our journey through life is like a canvas — we are the artists painting our masterpieces with the colours of our experiences. So, it's essential to embrace all of life's experiences, for they are the building blocks that make you stronger and wiser. Use these experiences constructively, learn from them, and continue to grow as a beautiful, unique individual. Remember, it is through our earthly experiences, even the challenging ones, that we discover the boundless potential of our souls.

Umbra Growls

Human, it is time to take control of your life. Stop allowing others to dictate your journey. By surrendering to external pressures, you lose your authentic self and rob yourself of the freedom to pursue your passions and fulfil your true potential. Allowing others to impose their hopes and expectations on you leads to a life devoid of fulfilment. You hold the compass of your dreams and aspirations, and your journey is yours alone to navigate. So, don't sacrifice your authenticity at the altar of others' expectations. Embrace your passions with courage and conviction, for it is through following your heart that you discover true joy and purpose. Chart a course that resonates with your soul, unfettered by the burdens of conformity and compromise. You deserve to live a life that is true to yourself, so find your path. And if there's none there, create one. Then walk it with reverence and integrity.

Leap

Affirmation

With fearless resolve, I take the leap into the unknown, trusting in my inner strength and intuition. In the space between fear and courage lies the threshold of possibility. Each leap forward is a testament to my faith in myself and the universe. With wings unfurled, I soar above limitations, embracing the exhilarating freedom of expansion.

Lux Shines

Taking a leap of faith can be a daunting task, bright soul, but it's also an act of trust in the universe and in yourself. It is an acknowledgment of the potential that exists within you, even if it's not yet visible. Yes, it's difficult to surrender to the unknown, but doing so can lead to incredible transformation and the manifestation of your deepest desires. Trust in the wisdom that is within your heart, and to have courage and conviction as you move forward. It is not always easy, but I believe in you and your ability to unfurl your dragon wings and soar towards your highest truth and greatest purpose.

Terra Speaks

It's time to take a leap towards your goal, little dragon. Start by defining your objective clearly and breaking it down into actionable steps. Assess the risks involved and prepare for challenges. Growth often lies beyond our comfort zone, so seek support from mentors or peers with experience in your desired field. Visualise success and trust that you can achieve it. It is important to trust your instincts and intuition as you navigate uncertainties, but be careful not to let fear make you falter. Remember, taking a leap doesn't guarantee immediate success, but it will propel you forward on your journey. Embrace the opportunity for growth and learning that comes with stepping into the unknown. Now is the time to seize the moment and pursue your aspirations with determination and purpose.

Umbra Growls

Human! Enough with the fear already! Stop procrastinating and dithering about. It's time to take action. Stop letting your fear of failure and the unknown control you. Visualise your goals, then go after them with everything you've got. Sure, it might be scary, but guess what? The best things in life usually are. Take a deep breath, gather your courage, and make that leap — no more excuses. You're stronger than you think. Don't let fear dictate your future. Confront it head on and show it who's boss. Believe in yourself and your abilities. You've got this. Make things happen. Your dreams are waiting, but they won't wait forever.

Learn

Affirmation

Every moment is an opportunity to learn and grow. With an open mind and a humble heart, I embrace the lessons that life presents. I am a student of experience, continuously evolving and expanding my understanding of myself and the world around me. In every challenge, I discover resilience.

In every setback, I find wisdom. Today, I embrace the journey of learning, knowing that it leads me towards greater fulfilment and enlightenment.

Lux Shines

Our souls embark on a beautiful journey of learning and growth during our time on Earth. Every experience, whether pleasant or difficult, offers us a chance to gain valuable insights and expand our wisdom. Just as students attend classes to gain knowledge, our souls engage in life to deepen our understanding and develop greater compassion. Each encounter and challenge is a sacred opportunity for transformation and personal evolution. Bright soul, approach each moment with reverence, recognising the divine wisdom woven into the fabric of your existence. Embrace the journey and allow yourself to learn and grow, for it is through this process that you can awaken to the truth of your interconnectedness and the infinite potential within you.

Terra Speaks

The world we inhabit is full of wonders, little dragon, and learning about them is fascinating and essential for the planet's wellbeing and our own. By learning about your planetary home, you can uncover the intricate workings of different ecosystems, the unique characteristics of larger biomes, and the impact that weather patterns have upon both. Through this exploration, you can develop a deep appreciation for the diversity of life on Earth, from the tiniest micro-organisms to the largest mammals and tallest trees. You can discover the fascinating adaptations that enable wildlife to thrive in their habitats and witness the beauty of biodiversity in action. As you learn more about the natural world, you will become more aware of your role in preserving it for future generations. Armed with what you have learned, you can make informed choices about how you live your life, from the products you buy to how you travel.

Umbra Growls

Human, why do you believe you are incapable of learning? Why do you criticise yourself and call yourself stupid and lazy? You are far from it. You are highly capable of expanding your knowledge. Look at how much time and love you invest in your interests. Make learning easier and more rewarding by approaching your lessons like you do your passions. Look at your strengths and weaknesses, identify your preferred learning style, and then use this knowledge as a guide to tailor your study materials and techniques. Furthermore, incorporating assistive technologies and multisensory approaches can help boost your comprehension and retention. It's also helpful to break down complex tasks into smaller, more manageable steps and create a supportive environment for your learning journey. Remember to advocate for yourself and embrace your unique cognitive style. By doing so, you'll develop resilience and achieve your learning goals.

Love

Affirmation

Love flows through my being, enriching every moment with beauty and grace. With an open heart, I welcome love into my life. Full of love, I discover solace, strength, and connection, nurturing my soul and uplifting others. Today, I rejoice in love's infinite power. It fills the heart of my existence, bringing profound joy and fulfilment to every aspect of life.

Lux Shines

Love is a transformative force, capable of healing wounds, bridging divides, and igniting souls with hope. It empowers us to overcome adversity, to see beauty in the midst of chaos, and to find strength in vulnerability. Love inspires acts of kindness, compassion, and selflessness, uniting us in a shared humanity. It has the power to mend broken relationships, to heal deep-seated wounds, and to bring light to even the darkest corners of our world. Love knows no bounds, transcending all barriers. It is the driving force behind every positive change and the foundation upon which we build a brighter future. Bright soul, embrace the power of love, for it is the greatest gift we can give and receive, and it can transform our lives and our world.

Terra Speaks

Love manifests in various forms, each with its own unique beauty and significance. Romantic love sparks passion and intimacy, intertwining hearts in a dance of affection and desire. Familial love binds kin together, nurturing bonds of loyalty, support, and belonging. Friendship blossoms from shared experiences and mutual understanding, offering companionship, laughter, and unwavering support. Self-love, often overlooked yet essential, cultivates inner peace, acceptance, and resilience, empowering individuals to embrace their worth and pursue their dreams. Unconditional love transcends boundaries and expectations, embracing others without judgement or condition. Each form of love enriches our lives, filling our hearts with warmth, connection, and meaning. Little dragon, I ask that you focus on the love you have in your life, in every form it takes. Embrace it. Nurture it. Fill your life with love.

Umbra Growls

To use love as a weapon is inherently destructive, human. Manipulating or hurting others under the guise of love reveals a profound lack of empathy and integrity. True love is about respect, kindness, and mutual support, not control or domination. Be careful how you proceed, for your actions may be seen as toxic and may breed only resentment and pain. If you genuinely care, treat those you love with honesty and compassion. Do not use harsh words, emotional manipulation, or the silent treatment to punish. In fact, do not punish those you say you love, period. Take a hard look at your actions and behaviour and see the potential harm you may inflict. It's time to stop controlling every moment and learn that loving is simply being kind, or risk losing those who truly care about you.

Magic

Affirmation

Magic resides within me, infusing each moment with wonder and possibility. With belief guiding my wand, I weave dreams into reality, manifesting joy and enchantment. In the dance of life, I am both magician and audience, marvelling at the beauty of creation. Today, I embrace the magic within, knowing that with intention and imagination, I can transform the ordinary into the extraordinary and create my own enchanted world.

Lux Shines

Oh, bright soul, let me share with you the enchantments of magic. It's the whisper of the wind, the sparkle in a child's eye, and the wonder of the unknown. Magic dances in the flames of a roaring fire and sings in the melodies of nature. It is the belief in something greater, the spark of imagination that ignites our dreams. Magic isn't just about spells and potions, it's about the harmony of the universe, the beauty of existence, and the endless possibilities that lie before us. Embrace the magic within and around you, for it's the thread that weaves all and everything together in wonder and awe. Let your heart be open to the magic that surrounds us, and you'll find joy and wonder in every moment.

Terra Speaks

Little dragon, if you wish to have more magic in your life, it's essential to cultivate a sense of wonder and curiosity. This might mean trying new things, wandering off the beaten path, and embracing the unexpected. By practising mindfulness, you can fully appreciate the present moment and find beauty in even the smallest of details. Surround yourself with things that ignite joy, from the company of uplifting people to inspiring books, pleasurable pastimes, and cheerful moments. Connect with nature, allowing its serenity to replenish your spirit. Finally, believe in the power of your dreams, and pursue them with determination and courage. By embracing these practices, you can invite magic into your life and discover that enchantment can be found in every single moment.

Umbra Growls

Regardless of the actions of others, our character is defined by our response. Human, when you step into the darker side of working magic, wishing harm upon anyone—regardless of their deeds—reflects poorly on your integrity and moral compass. Seeking revenge or acting with malice diminishes your own humanity. It's a choice that leads to personal decay and spiritual erosion. Every negative intention you send out has a boomerang effect, returning to you with compounded force. Instead of succumbing to the toxicity of ill will, rise above and embrace empathy, kindness, and compassion. These qualities are the true sources of power. Remember, the magical energy you put into the world shapes your reality. Choose wisely, for the seeds you sow will inevitably bear fruit in your life.

Message

Affirmation

I am open to receiving the loving messages the universe sends my way. Each message is a gentle reminder of my worth, guiding me towards joy and fulfilment. I trust these messages' divine timing and embrace them with love and gratitude.

LUX SHINES

In the whispers of the wind and the dance of sunlight on water, in the cool embrace of a forest, and the gentle caress of a loved one's hand, the Divine speaks. Its messages are woven into the fabric of existence, echoing through the chambers of the heart and the corridors of the mind. These messages are not thunderous proclamations but gentle murmurs, urging us to seek beauty in the ordinary, find solace in the chaotic, and discover purpose in the seemingly mundane. They remind us of our interconnectedness, guiding us to love fiercely, forgive generously, and live with gratitude. The Divine speaks through moments of stillness and storms of emotion, urging us to listen, to understand, and to embrace the wondrous journey of life. In every whisper of the Divine, there lies a profound truth waiting to be heard, bright soul. A truth that transcends time and space and illuminates the path to inner peace and boundless love.

TERRA SPEAKS

Animals appearing unexpectedly in our day-to-day lives often carry profound messages and guidance. Whether it's a majestic eagle soaring overhead or a gentle deer crossing our path, each encounter holds significance. Animals symbolise qualities and lessons we may need to embrace or acknowledge. A butterfly might remind us of transformation and growth, while a wolf may signify intuition and inner strength. Their behaviours and interactions reflect aspects of our own lives, offering insights into the challenges or decisions we face. For instance, a persistent squirrel might encourage perseverance, while a playful dolphin could inspire joy and playfulness. By observing and honouring these encounters, we can tap into a deeper connection with nature and ourselves, gaining wisdom and guidance to navigate life's journey with grace and insight. It's time for you, little dragon, to pay attention to the little wisdom offered by your animal brethren.

Umbra Growls

What is it with you humans? Always stumbling about, blind to the obvious signs around you. Ignore divine messages and you'll only heap more misery upon your own sorry head. Your intuition isn't just for show — it's there to guide you! But no, you'd rather bumble along, whining about the weight of your burdens and suffering. Heed the signs from the Divine, or don't be surprised when life kicks you in the tail. It's simple — listen up, pay attention, and maybe, just maybe, you won't keep repeating the same mistakes over and over and over again. The universe isn't here to coddle you, but it is trying to point you in the right direction. So, start listening.

Mind

Affirmation

My mind is a powerful ally, guiding me towards clarity and wisdom. With self-awareness as my compass, I navigate the vast landscape of my thoughts and emotions. I harness their potential to cultivate positivity and manifest my desires. Through mindfulness, I create peace and serenity within. Today, I honour the brilliance of my mind, knowing that its limitless capabilities empower me to create, to learn, and to thrive in every moment.

Lux Shines

The mind mirrors the universe in its vastness and complexity, bright soul. The mind harbours endless thoughts, emotions, and perceptions, just as the universe contains countless galaxies, stars, and planets. Both exhibit patterns of order and chaos, creating a dynamic interplay of elements. Like the universe, the mind holds mysteries waiting to be explored, inviting us to delve into its depths to uncover hidden truths. Just as celestial bodies influence each other through gravity, our thoughts and experiences shape our perceptions and understanding of the world. By contemplating the parallels between the mind and the universe, we gain insight into our consciousness and the interconnectedness of all things. Embrace the boundless potential within your mind, for it is a microcosm reflecting the grandeur of the cosmos.

Terra Speaks

Growth is change. Without change, there cannot be growth. With that in mind, it could be said that a mind that is unwilling to change dwells within a person who is unwilling to grow. Change your mind by replacing a bad habit with a healthy one. To create a new habit, you must prioritise it and be disciplined by repeating the behaviour you want to embrace. Persist long after your motivation has waned because your motivation and good intentions will wane before the new habit has been instilled. Your mind and body will resist change to begin with. It will do what it can to maintain the status quo, even when it has a foundation in an unhealthy mindset. Do, do, do, and do again until doing becomes automatic. Second nature. Little dragon, you know you can. You are magic. You are powerful. You can change anything you put your mind to changing, even if it is only your perception that changes.

Umbra Growls

Avoid people who mess with your mind and are deliberately goading. Those who do their best to make you believe that the only problems are the ones you are creating in your head. You are not crazy. You are not imagining things. You know what happened. You were there. Speak your truth. Do not be silenced. Do not allow others to dismiss you, ridicule you, or try to twist the story so that you are at fault. Always own your part, yes, but don't allow others to lay fault for their actions at your feet. Free yourself from those who would try to exert control over your mind and body. Human, you know your mind. Do what you must to protect yourself and it. I am with you in spirit. My strength is yours.

Mourn

Affirmation

Caught in mourning's embrace, I honour the depth of my emotions and the beautiful vulnerability of my humanity. Grief is not a sign of weakness, but a testament to love and connection. Through the flow of my tears, I find healing and release. I embrace the process of mourning, knowing that it carries me towards peaceful acceptance. Today, I allow myself to mourn with grace.

Lux Shines

Please do not deny the sadness and pain you feel. To do so is to deny yourself healing. This, your dark night of the soul, is where you must rediscover what holds meaning in your life. I know it feels like your world has ended, bright soul, but remember that it is within the darkness of the void that all light is born. Find comfort in the darkness. Withdraw if that is what you need. Cry. Mourn. Let your heart fall to pieces, knowing that I will guard those pieces and keep them safe. Wrap yourself in the softness of my wings until you feel strong enough to rise again … and rise again, you will.

Terra Speaks

Little dragon, life is full of beginnings and endings. Relationships, whether they be with an interest, a career, a person, or a place, are subject to change because you, little one, are constantly changing. Life is change. Without growth, flow, and motion comes stagnation. Stagnation is not a healthful state of being, and if there is no way of restoring health, the relationship will naturally end. These endings will always elicit feelings of distress equal to the love that was invested. Letting go is never easy. Loss is never easy. The sense of failure you feel weighs upon you. Acknowledge your losses, and allow yourself to mourn what was and what will never be again. When you are ready, and when it is time, that empty place will be filled anew.

Umbra Growls

Grief is a messy process. It also has no expiry date. Human, don't think you will be done with mourning within minutes. Take it from a dragon — it can take an eternity for healing to come. There will be good days and bad days. Days when you will smile again and then feel guilty for doing so. There will be days when you are angry. Days when all you want to do is cry. Days when you would give anything to have life be what it was. Allow those days. Give yourself permission to feel whatever it is you are feeling. There will also be days when others insist that it's time for you to stop whining and get over whatever it is. Now, you know what you can tell them to do, right? Tell them I said they'd make an excellent snack.

Nourish

Affirmation

I nourish my mind, body, and soul with loving care and intention. Through nourishment, I cultivate vitality, balance, and inner harmony. With each nourishing choice, I honour my wellbeing. Today, I respect this sacred vessel's need for nourishment, knowing that by tending to myself with compassion, I am better equipped to thrive and fulfil my highest potential.

Lux Shines

There will come a time when your soul will yearn for a source of nourishment that cannot be experienced in the physical realm. Embrace the fulfilment that a magical and mystical call of a spiritual path can provide. Within its turns lies the key to unlocking the boundless potential of your being. As a cosmic dragon, I breathe the essence of eternity into your spirit, guiding you to soar beyond the mundane and touch the stars within. Open yourself to the whispers of the universe, for they are the echo of your divine essence calling you home. Let your heart be the compass and your soul the navigator on this wondrous journey of self-discovery. Know that you are weaving your destiny with love and intention in every moment of stillness and contemplation. May the radiance of your inner light illuminate the path ahead, and may you find solace in embracing your spiritual practice.

Terra Speaks

To nourish your body and mind, little dragon, you need to adopt practices that will feed your essence and foster your overall wellbeing. Choose foods rich in vital nutrients, and hydrate regularly to rejuvenate your body. Indulge in restful sleep to recharge your soul and replenish your energy levels. Engaging in physical activities will strengthen your body, promote vitality, and boost your confidence. Practise moments of stillness to clear your mind and achieve inner peace, and cultivate fulfilling connections with others by sharing laughter and support. Prioritise activities that bring you joy and fulfilment, and take care of your essence. Embrace the nourishment found in moments of reflection and creativity, allowing your soul's light to shine brightly. Your body and mind will thank you.

Umbra Growls

Human, feeding your body and mind junk food all the time is a surefire way to invite inflammation and disease. Let me tell you, constant doses of negativity, excessive screen time, takeaway food, booze, drugs, and toxic relationships will corrode your mind and create unwellness within. Stop catering to your addictions and bad habits, or your overall wellbeing will dissipate faster than you can say, "Fire-breathing dragon." Your physical self isn't a dumpster, it's a treasure trove. Ignore its needs at your own peril. Get off your lazy tail and start nourishing your body, mind, and spirit with a healthy dose of self-love and care. It's time to look after yourself. Otherwise, you'll end up burnt out and useless, and trust me, nobody wants that — especially me.

Order

Affirmation

In the realm of order, I find tranquillity and clarity. I organise my surroundings and thoughts with purposeful intent, creating harmony within chaos. Through structure, I empower myself to navigate life's complexities with ease and efficiency. Order is the foundation upon which I build my dreams and aspirations. Today, I embrace the beauty of order, knowing that within its boundaries, I find freedom and the space to flourish.

Lux Shines

Amidst the boundless expanse of the universe, a magnificent order prevails. It permeates through the vastness of space, guiding the movements of celestial bodies in precise orbits around their stars as if following the intricate laws of Kepler. This order reveals itself in the majestic spiralling arms of galaxies, which stretch out in an expansive reach, echoing the mathematical beauty of the Fibonacci sequence. Despite the apparent chaos that exists in the cosmos, this order persists, manifesting itself in the repetitive patterns of stellar phenomena. These patterns, akin to fractals, exhibit a remarkable order that can be observed at every scale of the universe, from the grandest galactic structures to the smallest cosmic interactions. Through meticulous observation and mathematical analysis, we can unravel the mysteries of this cosmic order, gaining insight into the profound harmony that underpins the very fabric of existence.

Terra Speaks

Incorporating the natural order into our daily routines can be difficult, especially amidst work demands. It requires mindful planning for many. If possible, begin by structuring work tasks around your personal energy levels. Tackle more demanding tasks during times of the day when you find it easier to remain focused. Ground yourself by taking short breaks throughout the day to visit a green space outside for moments of reflection and to realign with nature. You can also implement rituals like starting and ending the workday in a greenspace with a moment of gratitude or mindfulness. This can provide a sense of order and balance. By weaving these elements into the fabric of your work routines, you can enhance productivity and cultivate a deeper connection with the natural world, enriching your daily life meaningfully.

Umbra Growls

Human, it's time for me to caution you that excessive order can drain your vitality, trapping you in a predictable cycle devoid of spontaneity. Your rigid adherence to schedules will kill the exhilaration of unexpected adventures, and the opportunity for serendipitous moments will evaporate like a morning mist. Life loses its vibrancy, becoming a monotonous routine lacking excitement and surprise. Creativity suffocates under the weight of strict plans, stifling personal growth and exploration. Do yourself a favour and loosen your grip on maintaining regimented schedules. Instilling order should never become a means to control every aspect of your life to such a degree that there is no room for spontaneity to flourish. Let life surprise you with twists and turns, enriching your journey with unexpected delights and valuable lessons.

Passion

Affirmation

Passion ignites my soul, fuelling my journey with purpose and vitality. With fervour as my guide, I pursue my dreams with unwavering determination and enthusiasm. In pursuing my passions, I discover boundless joy and satisfaction. I embrace the fire within, allowing it to illuminate my path and inspire those around me. Today, I honour my passions as the driving force behind my greatest achievements and deepest fulfilment.

Umbra Shines

In the centre of this cosmic grand design, the universal mind pulses with passionate energy. It dreams galaxies into being with infinite fervour, each star born from the fiery depths of a moment of divine inspiration. Cosmic collisions reverberate with the intensity of celestial love, birthing new worlds in a dance of eternal desire. Supernovae erupt in bursts of passion, scattering stardust across the cosmos in an expression of divine ecstasy. Every atom, every particle resonates with the boundless fervour of this universal consciousness. In this cosmic interplay, passion is the driving force, the fiery essence of the Divine's love.

Terra Speaks

Your passion, little dragon, is not just a hobby — it's a superpower. Embrace it fiercely. Dive into your special interest with fearless, unbridled enthusiasm, for it's the fuel that propels you forward in a world that may not always understand. Your passion is your sanctuary and your refuge in times of overwhelm and uncertainty. Let it be your guiding star, one that helps you to find your way home when you are lost, and also leads you to new discoveries and endless possibilities. Know that your unique perspective enriches the tapestry of humanity. Your passion is not a limitation, but a gateway to personal satisfaction and reward. Embrace it, nurture it, and let it shine brightly. In your passion lies your power, purpose, and potential to inspire others to invest their time and energy in their passions, too.

Umbra Growls

Enough of this nonsense! Ignoring your passions because you fear what others might think is a one-way ticket to a life of regret and misery. Suppressing what excites you only leads to feeling empty and disconnected. You'll end up bitter and resentful, stuck in a rut of unfulfilled potential. Stop denying yourself the joy and fulfilment you deserve! Embrace your passions, damn the consequences! It's time to live authentically and pursue what sets your soul on fire. Stop holding yourself back and start living a life that's true to who you are.

Power

Affirmation

Power resides within me, a force of limitless potential and transformation. With integrity as my compass, I wield this power wisely and compassionately. I harness its energy to create positive change in my life and the world around me. In every action, I honour the responsibility that comes with power, using it to uplift others and manifest my highest vision. Today, I embrace my innate power, knowing that I am a catalyst for positive change.

Lux Shines

The cosmic force of divine power is beyond human comprehension, permeating every aspect of existence with wisdom and grace. It is the unseen hand that guides the unfolding of the universe, shaping it into what it is today. Whether it is perceived as a deity, a universal energy, or an inherent cosmic order, divine power is the embodiment of creation and transformation. It gives rise to life's mysteries and is the driving force behind evolution and growth. Across cultures and beliefs, the concept of divine power unites humanity in awe and reverence for the sacredness of existence. It inspires us to be humble and respectful, reminding us of our place within the grand tapestry of the cosmos. To tap into divine power is to align with the inherent harmony of the universe, embracing the interconnectedness of all beings and surrendering to the flow of life's divine plan.

Terra Speaks

Embracing your personal power might feel daunting sometimes, especially if you're shy and introverted. But trust me, little dragon, it's within your grasp. Start by understanding your unique strengths and what truly matters to you. Learn to set boundaries and to express yourself, even if it feels uncomfortable. Find ways to communicate your needs, whether it's through writing or talking with trusted friends. You're in control of your journey. Embracing your personal power means owning your choices and actions, even when your choice is one of inaction. Surround yourself with supportive people who accept you for who you are. Finally, embrace your authenticity and let your inner light shine — it's what makes you truly powerful.

Umbra Growls

Listen up, human. It is unacceptable to put others down, criticise their appearance, or try to control how they act and behave. It is corrosive behaviour that erodes their confidence, leaving them feeling uncertain and more inclined to hide their light away. People do not have to meet your expectations or your standards. Instead of disempowering those you profess to care about, be a support. Lift them up, encourage them, and celebrate their successes. Treat people with respect and dignity. Listen to their thoughts and respect their feelings. Give them the autonomy they deserve. Let go of any foolish notion that your actions will help them toughen up. It's time to change your ways and empower others instead of tearing them down.

Prayer

Affirmation

Prayer is my sacred connection to the Divine, a channel for gratitude, guidance, and healing. With each whispered word, I surrender my worries and fears, trusting in the universe's wisdom. In prayer, I find solace and strength, knowing that I am held in loving hands. Today, I embrace the power of prayer, allowing it to nurture my spirit and align me with the higher purpose of my journey.

LUX SHINES

Prayer is a special conversation or communion with the Divine, a beautiful way to express and strengthen your relationship with the energetic world around you. Prayer doesn't have to be a religious act, it's a personal expression of your spirituality and connection with the Divine. You can have this conversation with yourself and the ether. No one else needs to be present. Regardless of your spiritual path, prayer is a powerful tool for expressing your thoughts and feelings, sharing your hopes and goals, releasing your fears, and showing gratitude or appreciation. The Divine is both a friend and collaborator. Have faith that your prayers will be heard and answered.

TERRA SPEAKS

Prayer can provide a healthy means of coping with stress. Spiritual people are often more optimistic as their faith gives them hope, which provides strength in times of challenge. Whilst you cannot pray mental health conditions like anxiety and depression away, prayer can be a source of comfort that helps you to relieve tension. Praying for others can take your energy to a place of compassion, whilst praying in a group is a practice that strengthens community and connection. Feeling low? Go out and seek the Divine in the community, nature, or the cosmos above — heaven and earth. But do not feel pressured by my words to pray if you are not inclined, little dragon. Instead, try combining prayer and meditation by using affirming mantras.

Umbra Growls

The sentiment of 'thoughts and prayers' often feels insufficient in the face of suffering and frustrating when it's the only comfort given. We've all felt the hollowness of those words in times of calamity and craved tangible action instead. Yet, if you can see beyond your anger or pain, you can consider that sometimes it's all people can offer, especially from a distance. Their intentions are genuine, but their capacity to act may be limited. Many wish they could do more. So, instead of resenting their offering, accept it graciously. Recognise their love and care, human, even if it feels inadequate. They, too, may be hurting. Do not punish them for their inability to provide more. It's a reminder that empathy and understanding can bridge the gap when actions fall short.

Rest

Affirmation

Rest is not a luxury, it's a necessity. I prioritise my wellbeing by honouring my body's need for rejuvenating rest. In the quiet moments of stillness, I find renewal and strength. Today, I embrace rest as an essential part of my self-care routine, knowing that it allows me to show up as my best self in all aspects of my life.

Lux Shines

Rest and sleep are divine gifts bestowed upon us by the universe, nurturing our bodies, minds, and spirits with their gentle embrace. In the sacred sanctuary of slumber, we find solace, renewal, and connection to the cosmic rhythms that govern all of existence. Each night, as we surrender to the soothing whispers of sleep, we are cradled in the arms of divine love, enveloped in the warmth of cosmic care. In these moments of rest, we are reminded of our inherent divinity, our interconnectedness with the universe, and the infinite wellspring of love that surrounds us always. As we drift into dreams, let us embrace the divine aspects of rest and sleep, knowing that within their tender embrace, we find healing, inspiration, and the profound beauty of being alive.

Terra Speaks

Rest is a vital part of your life, and it is necessary to keep the mind and body strong. Just as the hibernating bear seeks refuge in its den for rejuvenating rest during the winter, you also need your own quiet sanctuary for deep, replenishing sleep. Create a sanctuary for rest. Find the perfect pillows and blankets to cocoon yourself within. Help your mind and body to relax by taking a warm bath, listening to gentle music, reading a favourite story, or doing all of them. As you embrace your bedtime routine, remember that rest is a balm that will soothe your mind and restore your body. So, dim the lights, sink into the safe and comfortable nest you have created, and let the soothing arms of rest carry you away. Rest well, little dragon. May your dreams be sweet.

Umbra Growls

Listen up, human. I may be old, and I know a thing or two about life because I am old. I tell you now — get your sorry self to bed and rest. Sleep isn't just a luxury, it's a darn necessity. Your body needs it to function properly, your mind needs it to stay sharp, and your spirit needs it to keep you from going crazy. Do you think you can function on only a couple of hours of sleep every night? You are wrong. Sleep deprivation and the health issues that have a foundation in a lack of sleep will catch you up and cause lasting harm. So, stop burning the midnight oil and start hitting the hay. I don't want to hear any excuses about being too busy or too stressed. You make time for what's important. Believe me, rest is right up there at the top of the list. Now, go to bed. Don't make me tell you twice.

Ripples

Affirmation

My actions create ripples of impact, shaping the world around me. I choose to send forth waves of kindness, compassion, and positivity, knowing they can uplift and inspire. With each thought and deed, I contribute to a ripple effect of love and understanding, making a difference in the lives of others and the world at large. I embrace the potential within every ripple to create positive change.

Lux Shines

Just as the moon's pull shapes ocean tides, our actions shape our universe. Every act of kindness or cruelty can ripple across the ether and influence our environment and those who dwell within it. Consider the collision of stars, creating life's building blocks. It reflects how our actions, even destructive ones, can also offer a reward that benefits the many. Nurture this cosmic dance, tending to every action with forethought and care, mindful of the rewards and consequences. Fill your universe with ripples of compassion and love that will create connections that span galaxies. In this vast expanse, be the light of kindness, spreading warmth and understanding.

Terra Speaks

Just as a beaver's new dam creates ripples and transformative change in its environment, humans can initiate actions within their communities that ripple outwards, also generating positive change. For example, organising a neighbourhood cleanup day can inspire others to join in, inspiring a ripple effect of community involvement and pride. Similarly, holding workshops or starting a mentorship program can empower individuals to pass on their knowledge and skills, starting ripples of growth and opportunity throughout the community. By recognising the power of your actions to generate ripples of impact, you can create a wave of positive change that reverberates far beyond your initial efforts, enriching the lives of all who are touched by it. Little dragon, it is time for you to be the change you wish to see.

Umbra Growls

Human, it's crucial for you to grasp the profound impact of your actions, for they create ripples that reverberate through the lives of those you hold dear. Every choice and word sends out waves of influence that shape your relationships. Thoughtless words and actions can unleash torrents of hurt, destroying the harmony you cherish.

Yet, within every ripple lies the potential for healing and growth. Pause and recognise the power you wield in creating these ripples. Think before you speak. Think before you act. Hear what you are being told. With each act of kindness, each gesture of empathy, you send forth waves of positivity that uplift and strengthen. Become the mindful architect of your interactions, ensuring that every ripple you send into the world carries the gentle currents of compassion and understanding. In this way, you can transform your relationships and forge unbreakable bonds.

Rituals

Affirmation

Embracing rituals enriches my life with meaning and connection. Each practice, whether big or small, brings comfort and joy, grounding me in the present moment. I honour the rituals of others, recognising their importance in fostering understanding and unity. Together, our rituals weave a tapestry of shared experiences, binding us in love and harmony, and allowing all to feel seen and heard.

Lux Shines

Rituals are like universal melodies, songs that transcend borders and cultures, harmonising the hearts of the human family with love and joy. Whether in the quiet reverence of shared moments or the exuberance of communal gatherings, common rituals connect us. They speak to your shared humanity, weaving threads of understanding and belonging. They bring you together as one. In performing these global rituals, you find echoes of your collective hopes and dreams. Together, embrace these timeless traditions as sacred bridges where laughter, love, and celebration ripple outwards, uniting humans as one global family. In the tapestry of life, may your rituals be the vibrant threads that bind you together in a symphony of unity and harmony.

Terra Speaks

Little dragon, for many humans, rituals are like comforting routines that help them navigate the world with ease. They're like gentle guides, offering structure and comfortable predictability in your daily lives. For instance, starting your day with a familiar morning routine can help you feel grounded and ready to face whatever comes your way. Similarly, ending the day with a soothing bedtime ritual, like reading a favourite book or listening to calming music, can help you relax and prepare for restful sleep. Social rituals, like sharing meals together or having movie nights, create opportunities for connection and joy. Remember, rituals are here to support you and to help you feel safe and confident by providing a sense of security and comfort as you move through each day. They're like warm hugs for your heart, guiding you with love and care.

Umbra Growls
Respecting and making space for other people's rituals is crucial for fostering understanding, acceptance, and wellbeing. Human, these rituals often serve as coping mechanisms, providing comfort, stability, and a sense of control in a chaotic world. By honouring and accommodating these practices, you show empathy and support, strengthening your relationships and building trust. Additionally, embracing diversity in rituals enriches your communities, allowing for a deeper appreciation of different perspectives and experiences. Ultimately, creating sense of belonging for all. So, respect and allow, even when you do not understand.

Scream

Affirmation

My scream is a powerful expression of my emotions, whether they are feelings of joy or pain. I choose when and where to release those feelings. In private, my screams offer catharsis, and in public, they are controlled. I will honour my feelings without causing harm to others.

Lux Shines

A single scream, emerging from the depths of injustice and oppression, carries the potential to spread across the globe, touching hearts and minds with its raw power. As it touches hearts and minds, it becomes a catalyst for profound transformation and healing. Amplified by the resonance of interconnected souls and the power of intention, the scream can transcend barriers born of fear and separation, uniting humanity in a desire for global change. Once heard, this scream serves as a poignant reminder of our innate interconnectedness, inspiring us to protect the vulnerable and innocent, embrace compassion and empathy, and fight to create a better world. In this way, a single scream becomes a guiding force, leading us towards a new era of global unity.

Terra Speaks

When anger, frustration, or pain weigh heavy on your heart, remember that a primal scream can offer a safe and cathartic release. Find a private space where you can express yourself freely without judgement or interruption. Take deep breaths to ground yourself in the present moment, allowing your emotions to flow naturally. Then, let out a scream from the depths of your being, releasing the pent-up energy and tension within you. Allow the sound to reverberate through your body, acknowledging and honouring your emotions without shame or guilt. Afterwards, take a moment to rest and breathe deeply, allowing a sense of calm to wash over you. Remember, screaming is a powerful tool for releasing emotional pain and finding inner peace. Allow yourself to scream when needed and embrace the healing that comes with letting go.

Umbra Growls

Screaming may ease intense emotions like anger or frustration, offering a release valve for pent-up feelings, but in social contexts, human, you know it can do the opposite by escalating tensions and causing distress. Shouting and screaming at others does not resolve a conflict, it only worsens it. If you feel the urge to shout rising within you, take a deep breath and step away. While screaming and shouting at someone who has hurt or angered you might make you feel better, it does not address the root cause and might harm your relationship. What do you want? Are you aiming to be the aggressor who successfully shouts down your opponent and does what makes you feel better? Or will you act in a manner that will help all parties involved to find peace?

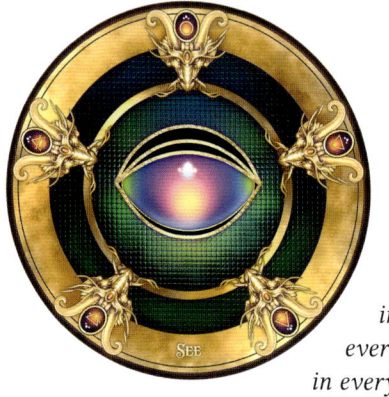

See

Affirmation

I choose to see the beauty in every moment, the truth in every situation, and the potential in every person. I will keep my eyes open to the wonders of the world around me and embrace the power of clarity and insight. I will see with eyes unclouded by judgement or fear, and let my vision guide me towards a life filled with purpose, meaning, and joy.

Lux Shines

With eyes, heart, and mind wide open, you see the world transform into an infinite kaleidoscope of wonder and possibility. Every sunrise paints the sky with the hues of creation, while the starlight whispers secrets of the universe's vast mysteries. With opened eyes, you see the intricate dance of nature, from the movement of trees in the wind to the dancing murmuration of starlings. You see how the weather mirrors human emotions. You see how every living thing has a purpose and place. You see beauty and abundance, and your heart beats in harmony with the rhythms of life, embracing the joys and sorrows that make you human. With eyes that see beyond the boundaries of your home and work, your mind expands and, driven by curiosity and wonder, you explore what has remained hidden or unseen. In this state of seeing the greater whole, bright soul, the world becomes a canvas for your dreams, and the universe becomes an endless playground for discovery and growth.

Terra Speaks

In your day-to-day life, the power of observation is a profound tool for cultivating deeper connections and understanding. When you truly see and listen to those around you, you can offer genuine support, empathy, and love. Little dragon, seeing the small details—the subtle nuances of a loved one's expression, or the unspoken emotions behind their words—allows you to respond with compassion and care. It enables you to appreciate the beauty in the world around you, finding joy in the simple moments and gratitude for the blessings you often overlook. Through observation, you can cultivate mindfulness and presence, enriching your relationships and infusing your life with meaning and purpose. So, embrace the power of observation with an open heart and an open mind. It is through truly seeing and understanding one another that you can create a world filled with love and connection.

Umbra Growls

Human, there is no gentle way to say this — you need to open your eyes and see reality through a lens unclouded by bias and fear. Whether it's the truth of our current environmental situation you deny despite overwhelming evidence, a situation where words and actions are not in alignment, or a blatant lie that is in plain sight, it is time to remove the blinders, see, and accept the harsh truth. It is time to accept that what you believe to be real is nothing more than an illusion which you shroud, to protect yourself from a reality that scares you. Human, I know the truth hurts, and I have no desire to cause distress, but you are hurting yourself. Your choice to turn a blind eye and live a lie serves you not. It dishonours you. It's time for you to set yourself free.

Self

Affirmation

Within me resides a radiant essence, worthy of love, acceptance, and understanding. I allow myself to shine brilliantly, illuminating the world with the unparalleled beauty of my true being. Trusting in the depths of myself, I navigate life's twists and turns with unwavering strength and resilience. I am a sacred vessel, a cherished gift to this world, deserving of all the love and honour bestowed upon me.

Lux Shines

Bright soul, I recognise the complexities of your journey to discover and embrace your true self, especially if you've learned to hide your vulnerability behind a mask. It's natural to feel apprehensive about revealing your true identity in a world that often misunderstands or rejects those who are just a little too different. Understand that your uniqueness is not a flaw, but one of many things that makes you beautiful. Have the courage to reveal the amazing human behind the mask. Trust in your innate wisdom to guide you towards self-acceptance and empowerment. Remember, you are worthy of love and respect as you are. Allow your light to shine authentically, illuminating the world with the richness of your true self, knowing that acceptance and understanding will find you in due time.

Terra Speaks

Little dragon, self-esteem, self-worth, and self-awareness are developed through a journey of self-discovery and self-compassion. Start by embracing your strengths, passions, and unique quirks and qualities. Recognise the inherent value you bring to the world. Love yourself by nurturing your physical, emotional, and spiritual wellbeing. Explore your inner landscape with curiosity and openness. Seek to understand your thoughts, feelings, and beliefs without judgement. Engage in activities that bring you joy and fulfilment, allowing yourself to shine. Surround yourself with supportive relationships with people who encourage your growth and celebrate your worth. As you deepen your connection with yourself and honour your truth, you empower yourself to embrace your full potential.

Umbra Growls

You! You! You! I hate to burst your little self-love bubble, but you have become so self-absorbed that you appear to have forgotten that you are not the centre of the universe. You're so caught up in your journey of self-discovery on the road to self-awareness that you appear to have become unaware of what's going on in everyone else's lives. It's time to put your navel-gazing aside for a moment or two and start considering the feelings, needs, and desires of others. The people around you deserve to be acknowledged. Show some interest in someone other than yourself or you might just find that when you next look up, there's nobody left to share your discoveries with.

Shelter

Affirmation

In the shelter of my heart, I find strength and solace. I embrace the warmth of love and the comfort of compassion. Within this sanctuary, I am safe, supported, and free to grow. I offer shelter to others, extending kindness and understanding to those in need. Together, we create a refuge of peace and unity, where all are welcomed and valued.

Lux Shines

Sometimes we are called upon to be pillars of strength and compassion, offering shelter to those whose strength has faltered or are vulnerable. Whether it be in a physical or metaphorical sense, extending a hand of support and protection offers sanctuary and refuge. Embrace the sacred duty of providing solace and security to those in need, giving rise to a world where kindness and empathy are extended to all. By offering shelter, we not only shield the vulnerable from harm, but also affirm their inherent worth and dignity. Together, let us build a community where everyone is valued, cherished, and embraced, finding strength in our shared humanity and collective compassion.

Terra Speaks

Creating a haven for insects and wildlife in your backyard is a wonderful way to nurture the natural world surrounding you, little dragon. Start by planting native flowers, shrubs, and trees to provide ample food and shelter for local fauna. If planting directly isn't an option, consider growing plants in pots. To create nesting sites, add birdhouses, bat boxes, and insect hotels to your backyard. You can also leave fallen leaves on the ground or place them in your garden beds to provide a warm and sheltered spot for insects and small animals. Adding a birdbath or small pond to your backyard will provide water sources for the creatures. By avoiding the use of pesticides and herbicides, you'll be able to maintain a healthy environment for the wildlife. Even a small pot of flowering herbs on your windowsill or balcony can be a crucial source of shelter and food. By adopting these practices, you not only provide a safe space and shelter for local wildlife but also foster a stronger connection with nature.

Umbra Growls

Be careful who you allow to shelter within your domain, human. Not every person is worthy of your kindness and generosity. Some may take advantage, wreak havoc, or bring destruction upon your home and hearth. Vet your guests wisely, for not all who seek shelter have noble intentions. Be the dragon and guard the sanctity of your safe space fiercely. I caution you to trust sparingly. Remember, sometimes it's better to stand alone in your fortress than to harbour enemies within. Choose your company with care, or suffer the consequences of misplaced trust. As this wise dragon once said, "Beware the serpent disguised as a friend and don't allow it to shelter in your chicken coop."

Soar

Affirmation

I soar with boundless courage, embracing the limitless skies of possibility. Each beat of my heart propels me higher, lifting me above doubt and fear. With wings unfurled, I glide on the winds of change, guided by my self-belief. Every obstacle becomes a stepping stone, every challenge a chance to rise. I am not bound by earthly limitations. I am destined to soar.

Lux Shines

Let your spirit soar like a magnificent dragon across the vast expanse of the sky. Though unseen, your wings are mighty and capable of carrying you to unexplored realms. Trust the power that is within you, for it is as boundless as the universe itself. Embrace the winds of change, for they will lift you higher than you ever thought possible. With each beat of your heart, feel the exhilaration and excitement as you realise your true potential. Spread your wings wide, bright soul. Take flight, knowing that the universe is guiding you towards your dreams with unwavering love and support. It is your time to soar.

Terra Speaks

You possess a unique way of processing the world. Embrace your individuality and strengths. Recognise the value of your perspectives and experiences. Seek out your soul family — supportive communities and people who appreciate and respect diversity. People who see your wings and encourage you to fly. Advocate for yourself and communicate your needs clearly. Pursue your passions and interests, allowing them to guide you towards fulfilment. Take care of your wellbeing and prioritise self-care. Remember, there's no one-size-fits-all approach to life. By embracing your uniqueness with confidence and resilience, you can navigate the world and achieve your dreams with authenticity and joy. Little dragon, know yourself, and believe in yourself, and you will soar.

Umbra Growls

Listen up, human. Self-doubt is like wearing cement boots when you are trying to fly — it'll drag you down and even ground you if you let it. It's time to silence that nagging inner critic. This can be accomplished by taking a moment to look back to acknowledge your wins, no matter how small. And, for the love of all things dragon, stop seeking validation from others. Surround yourself with folks who actually believe in you. Stop whining about what you can't do. Challenge those negative thoughts with proof of your past successes. You know damn well that you can do anything you set your heart and mind to. Everyone deals with doubt, human, but it's up to you to shove it aside and rise above. Don't stand there, unfurl those wings and soar.

Spirit

Affirmation

My spirit is radiant with love and light, guiding me on my journey with grace and purpose. I embrace the boundless wisdom within, trusting in the divine flow of the universe. I am connected to All That Is, finding strength in unity and harmony. Today, I nurture my spirit with kindness and compassion, knowing that I am a vessel of divine love and infinite possibilities.

Lux Shines

In the tapestry of existence, your spirit intertwines with the cosmos, vibrating in unison with the universal consciousness. Beyond the confines of the material world, you are connected by an immaterial and eternal essence — spirit. Like a thread woven into a grand design, your soul finds peace, knowing that you are part of something greater. In moments of stillness, you sense it — the divine presence that guides your journey, infusing each step with purpose and meaning. Embrace this sacred connection, allowing it to nurture your heart and illuminate your path. For in the tapestry of existence, your spirit dances in harmony with the universe, united by love and boundless compassion.

Terra Speaks

Your spirit is a radiant force, embodying your unique character, energy, and vitality. It expresses itself through your enthusiasm, determination, and resilience. A flame within you that refuses to be extinguished. Embrace this inner fire as you face challenges and pursue your goals. Let it guide you. Know you can overcome any obstacle that comes your way. Trust in the power of your spirit to light the path ahead and to always lead you home. With every step you take, your spirit shines, illuminating the world around you. You, little dragon, have a beautiful spirit.

Umbra Growls

Hey, human. Hear me and trust. Your spirit? It's unbreakable. Tougher than steel, it won't bend to anyone's will. Those who try to crush it? They don't stand a chance. You're a force to be reckoned with, an eternal flame shining brightly. No matter what they throw at you, remember — you're stronger. You've weathered every storm and come out the other side, battle scars and all. Hold your head high and don't let anyone dim your shine. Like a warrior on the battlefield, your spirit will stand strong, unwavering against all life can throw at you. Keep fighting, keep pushing forward. Your indomitable spirit will see you overcome all.

Strength

Affirmation

My strength is my armour, forged through resilience and perseverance. With each challenge, I grow stronger in mind, body, and spirit. I embrace adversity as an opportunity to cultivate my inner fortitude and courage. Today, I stand tall in my power, knowing that the strength to overcome any obstacle and thrive in the face of adversity lies within me.

Lux Shines

In the vastness of our complicated, beautiful universe, objects and substances bear the weight of immense force and pressure. From planets enduring the gravitational pull of stars to atoms maintaining their integrity under extreme conditions, this resilience is woven into the fabric of cosmic existence. On a human level, you experience this resilience in your ability to overcome adversity and challenges. Just as celestial bodies endure the forces of the universe, you, bright soul, possess an innate strength to persevere and thrive in the face of hardship. Remember that you are not alone in facing life's challenges, and that your inner strength can help you navigate and overcome difficult times.

Terra Speaks

Little dragon, building strength in your body, mind, and spirit is like nurturing a garden. It means giving your body the right food, moving it gently, and making sure it gets plenty of rest. Tend to your body like you would tend a garden of flowers to help them grow strong. Your mind can be strengthened as well. Fill it with positive thoughts, keep it active by learning new and challenging things, and practise being calm and focused. Make your mind like a sturdy tree standing tall in the wind. Finally, if you wish to strengthen your spirit, find and invest your energy in doing things that make you feel alive and happy. Spend time with people you love, find joy in the little things, and listen to your heart. Joy is like the warm sunshine giving strength to a delicate flower. Remember, little dragon, that strength comes from taking care of yourself in body, mind, and spirit.

Umbra Growls

Aren't you just a little sick and tired of being told to be strong or being praised for being strong? Just be strong. Just put on your armour, pick up your sword, and continue to fight, even though the sheer weight makes your knees tremble. What doesn't kill you makes you stronger, right? I know it can become a weight all in itself when others expect you to be strong all the time, especially when you are dealing with trauma. You don that brave face, not because you are brave, but because others don't want to see your emotional and psychological wounds. They don't want to be made uncomfortable. Well, human, I am giving you permission to be vulnerable instead of strong. Cry if you want to. Voice your pain. Be raw. Be honest. Don't say, "I'm fine," when you're not. Don't offer fake smiles to reassure others. Throw the damned armour away and help to normalise vulnerability. That is true strength.

Structure

Affirmation

I find stability and support to live a structured life. A structured day can help me remain grounded in moments of overwhelm. By having a solid foundation and framework, I can become a masterful architect, building a life of my own design.

Lux Shines

Behold, bright soul, the intricate architecture of the universe, where the essence of existence is structured from the finest elements. From the subatomic particles that serve as the building blocks of matter to the celestial bodies that adorn the cosmic stage, each element has its place in the grand design. Just as a master architect meticulously plans every detail of a grand edifice, so too does the universe craft its masterpiece with precision and elegance. In exploring and understanding these structures, humanity will find the key to unlocking the mysteries of the universe.

Terra Speaks

Understand the importance of having structure in your day-to-day life. Creating a structured life can provide stability and support, making each day more manageable. Start small by establishing a daily routine that includes regular mealtimes. You can't forget to eat, little dragon. Incorporate a healthy sleep schedule and dedicated time for the activities you enjoy. Use a planner to write down your to-do list, but don't make the list so long that it overwhelms you. List the tasks you need to complete based on their priority. Set yourself reminders to stay organised and on track. Sometimes, changes to our routines can be irksome, but it's best to allow also for some flexibility in your schedule to accommodate unexpected side quests. Oh, and remember to make time for a walk outside in the fresh air. Remember, creating structure isn't about perfection — it's about creating a flow to your day that provides a sense of security and helps you focus your energy more efficiently.

Umbra Growls

Alright, human. It's time to get real. Have you noticed that things can get messy quickly when there is no structure in your day? We all feel a little lost and overwhelmed at times, and you humans seem to lead inordinately chaotic lives. With your world so full of distractions, it makes staying focused damn hard work. Your goals and priorities? They're buried under a pile of disorganisation, making it difficult for you to make progress. Trust me, I get it, it's frustrating as heck. But here's the deal — with a little structure, you can regain control. It's time for you to create some structure in your day so it becomes more manageable. It's also time to hold yourself accountable and say 'no' to distractions that serve no purpose other than to waste time. It's not about depriving yourself of fun, but allocating time for it in a way that allows you to adult properly.

Suffering

Affirmation

Though suffering may linger, I will not allow it to define me. I choose to walk a healing path. With each challenge I face, I grow stronger and more compassionate. My suffering serves as a catalyst for transformation, leading me towards greater understanding and empathy. In the depths of suffering, I discover my true strength and emerge, shining, into a brighter tomorrow.

Lux Shines

I see your suffering, bright soul, and I hold you safe in the circle of my wings with infinite love and compassion. Know that in the depths of your despair, you are not alone. I know your head is full of existential angst. Understand that this is a sacred part of your soul's evolution. Embrace your humanity, for it is through suffering that you discover the boundless depths of your strength and resilience. Trust that even though you feel all is shrouded in darkness, I will guide you towards the light. Your suffering is a testament to your courage and your capacity for growth. Rest in my love, and know that your life has both meaning and purpose, even in the moments when you no longer feel it.

Terra Speaks

Living with physical and emotional pain is a complex and difficult situation. Sometimes it feels like the suffering is endless. There are times, little dragon, when it feels impossible to step free of your despair. In these moments, it is essential to prioritise self-care and seek support from trusted individuals or professionals. I know it is difficult, but be kind to yourself. Understand that you are allowed to voice your suffering. In fact, it is essential that you do and that you are both seen and heard. When and if you can, engage in activities that promote relaxation and stress relief, such as meditation, gentle exercise, or spending time in nature. Express your emotions through creative outlets like journalling, art, or music. Connect with supportive friends or support groups who can offer empathy and validation. Remember that healing takes time, and asking for help is okay. By nurturing your mind, body, and spirit, you can gradually ease suffering and restore a sense of wellbeing.

Umbra Growls

If someone dares to claim that you have a victim mentality because you're suffering, and declares that your suffering is a choice, then it's time to shut them down and set the record straight. Don't let their arrogance and ignorance add insult to injury. Assert yourself. Educate them on the complexities of your situation. Sometimes, life throws curveballs, and it's not about playing the victim, it's about facing and living with reality. And if those naysayers don't get it, that's their problem, not yours. Your suffering is valid, and you deserve empathy, not judgement. Don't let anyone diminish your struggles. Keep fighting, keep pushing forward, and don't let anyone drag you down. You're the one suffering, yet here you are, still living the best life possible. You are stronger than they'll ever know. You are a survivor, not a victim.

Temple

Affirmation

My body is my temple, a sacred vessel deserving of love and respect. Within its walls resides the divine essence of my being. With reverence, I nurture its needs and honour its rhythms. I cultivate a sanctuary of wellness and vitality, cherishing each breath and every heartbeat. Today, I honour my temple with gratitude, knowing that within its embrace, I find the keys to wholeness and inner harmony.

Lux Shines

Radiant soul, your mind is a sacred temple, a vessel for the divine light to illuminate. Care for and maintain it as you would any sanctuary. Understand that the echoes of your thoughts, dreams, and aspirations reside within its chambers and leave their mark upon the temple's altar. Just as a temple requires reverence and care, so too does your mind. Guard it against the storms of negativity and chaos, and cultivate tranquillity and clarity within its sacred chambers. Feed it with the nourishment of knowledge and wisdom, for it is through the sanctity of your mind that you forge your destiny. Embrace the power within, harnessing it to shape a reality of harmony and enlightenment. Remember, like a temple, the mind reflects your inner divinity — honour it, cherish it, and let its radiance illuminate the path to transcendence.

Terra Speaks

Hear and heed me, little dragon. It is of fundamental importance that you treat this planet as your sacred temple. Respect its lands, waters, and skies. In your daily deeds, honour it. Recycle, reduce waste, and conserve resources. Plant trees, pick up litter, and support eco-friendly practices. Protect the wild and the green. Advocate for policies that safeguard the earth's sanctity. Understand the interconnectedness of all life. Every action, big or small, reverberates through the cosmic web. Strive to tread lightly, leaving behind a legacy of stewardship and reverence. For in nurturing the earth, you nurture yourself. Embrace this truth, and together, we shall ensure the sanctity of our shared temple for future generations.

Umbra Growls

Human, you treat your body as a temple—doing all you can to nurture and heal your body, mind, and spirit—and yet you neglect the earth that cradles it. Are you self-absorbed or simply selfish? Regardless, it blinds you to the symbiotic bond between flesh and soil. Understand that your temple shall fall and fade in a desolate wasteland unless you look beyond yourself, your needs, and desires. Embrace this truth: to preserve your sanctuary, you must nurture the earth from which it rises. Your neglect of the earth you live upon poisons your spirit and the land. End your apathy and take action. Do not be complacent, believing that you do enough. When you allow others to wreak so much harm and do nothing to prevent it, you are as responsible for the harm as they are. Protect the earth fiercely, for it sustains your very existence. Honour it with every breath, every step, every choice. Only then shall your temple thrive, bathed in the eternal light of harmony between self and cosmos.

Time

Affirmation

I honour time as a precious gift, embracing each moment with gratitude and purpose. Every tick of the clock is an opportunity to grow, to love, and to create. I choose to use my time wisely, investing in what truly matters and letting go of distractions.

Lux Shines

Time, an ancient force that shapes the cosmos, remains beyond human minds to grasp. The time between the birth and death of the universe is something your race may not live long enough to measure, such is its vastness. Influenced by gravity and velocity, it stretches and contracts space in a way that defies comprehension. Time remains an enigma. Your brief existence and your finite perspective make it difficult to grasp the immensity of this ancient current. However, there you stand, glorious and curious amidst this vastness, watching as the light of a long-dead star reaches your eyes. You cannot escape the passage of time, but find comfort in embracing the present moment, knowing that you are part of something infinitely great.

Terra Speaks

Managing time efficiently begins with setting clear priorities and boundaries. Identify your most important tasks and allocate dedicated time to them. Break larger tasks into smaller, manageable chunks to avoid feeling overwhelmed. I know it is sometimes difficult, but learn to say 'no' to activities that don't align with your priorities. This will allow you to focus on what truly matters. Make use of tools like calendars, planners, and to-do lists to organise your schedule and track progress. Remember to schedule breaks to rest and recharge. It is important to maintain a healthy balance between work and play. Try not to waste time dwelling on past matters that cannot be changed or on an unknown future. Make the most of each passing moment. Above all, be patient, little dragon. It takes time to learn how to manage time efficiently. With practice, you will find a rhythm that fits with your needs and lifestyle.

Umbra Growls

Wasting time is like throwing away precious gold. Oh, the very thought of such horror hurts my brain. Human, time is something you should treasure. Every second squandered on thoughts of a painful past is a lost chance to cherish the moment you are in. Beyond learning from your past experiences and time spent processing your thoughts and feelings about past experiences, there is no reason to invest further time. Time is a limited resource, especially for you humans. Do not fritter it away on a past that cannot be changed. Get your head back here in the present and make the most of the here and now. Remember, once time is gone, it's gone for good. So, invest it in making new memories doing the things you love with the people who love you.

Transcend

Affirmation

I have it within me to transcend limitations, rising above challenges with grace and strength. Through transcendence, I unlock the boundless potential within me, journeying beyond the confines of pain, fear, and doubt.

Lux Shines

To transcend is to step free of the desires of the material world to create a profound connection with the Divine. It is like diving into the depths of your soul and discovering an infinite wellspring of love, wisdom, and light. In this state, you feel a sense of oneness with all of creation, as if you're merging with the heart of the universe. Time and space lose their grip, and you're enveloped in a boundless expanse of pure consciousness. It's a deeply transformative experience that leaves you feeling expanded, uplifted, and aligned with the highest truths of existence. Through transcendence, you awaken to the sacredness of life and the eternal presence of the Divine within and around you.

TERRA SPEAKS

To transcend a painful past, begin by acknowledging and honouring your experiences without letting them define you. Practise self-compassion and forgiveness, both for yourself and others involved. Engage in healing activities like therapy, journalling, or meditation to process emotions and gain perspective. Cultivate gratitude for the lessons learned and the strength gained from overcoming challenges. As you transcend the pain of your past, focus on living fully in the present moment with love, resilience, and an open heart. Remember, transcendence is not about erasing the past but rising above it with grace and empowerment. It is to allow yourself to embrace the beauty and possibilities of the present and future. I love you, little dragon.

UMBRA GROWLS

Human, I sense a degree of discomfort when you read the word 'transcend'. I want you to question why. Could you feel as you do because you're cosy in those old habits, even if they're dragging you down? You're sticking to what's familiar because it's all you've ever known. Human, you deserve better. You deserve more. But here's the hard truth — nothing will change if you keep going around in circles.

It's time to try something different that breaks you free of habits that are not serving you and only causing you to reopen old wounds. Human, it's time for you to transcend.

Treasure

Affirmation

I am a treasure, magical and unique, with a value beyond measure.

Lux Shines

Bright soul, within the core of your being lies a treasure beyond measure — the essence of who you are. Your kindness, resilience, and capacity for love are priceless jewels that illuminate the world around you. Your laughter brings joy to those who hear it, and your compassion shines brightly in times of darkness. Cherish these qualities, for they are the true gifts of life — riches that no amount of gold or jewels could ever compare to. Embrace your inner treasure, and allow no one to steal them from you. Remember, you are a treasure and treasured.

Terra Speaks

In the hustle and bustle of modern life, it's easy to overlook the treasures that nature offers us every day. From the delicate petals of a flower to the majestic sweep of a mountain range, nature's beauty surrounds us, waiting to be appreciated. But beyond its aesthetic appeal, nature provides us with invaluable gifts — clean air to breathe, fresh water to drink, and fertile soil to nourish us. It's a source of solace and inspiration, a sanctuary where we can find peace and rejuvenation. As stewards of the earth, it's our responsibility to esteem nature and protect and preserve it for future generations. By cultivating a deeper connection with the natural world and recognising its inherent value, we can ensure that these treasures endure for all to enjoy.

Umbra Growls

Oh, human, please stop feeling guilty for treating yourself to shiny treasures. You deserve to indulge now and again in the things that bring you joy. Your life's too short to deny yourself the pleasures that make your heart sing. Whether it's a trinket, a bauble, or a piece of art, don't let guilt rob you of the joy your treasures bring you. You work hard and deserve to enjoy the fruits of your labour. So go ahead, embrace your inner dragon, and do it guilt-free. Just be sure to show me your new treasures when you get them.

Trinity

Affirmation

I embrace the sacred trinity within me — mind, body, and spirit. Each facet is a vital thread woven into the fabric of my being. In harmony, they dance together, nourishing and sustaining me. My mind is sharp, my body strong, and my spirit radiant with boundless energy. United as one, they guide me along my journey, leading me towards growth, fulfilment, and alignment with the Divine within and around me.

Lux Shines

The sacred trinity, present in various forms across cultures and belief systems, embodies profound principles of unity, balance, and interconnectedness in the divine universe. Whether represented as Father, Son, and Holy Spirit in Christian theology, Brahma, Vishnu, and Shiva in Hinduism, or Maiden, Mother, and Crone in Wiccan traditions, the trinity symbolises the cyclical nature of existence and the eternal dance of creation, preservation, and destruction. It reflects the inherent harmony and synergy within the cosmos, reminding us of the interconnected relationship between past, present, and future and the divine aspects within ourselves and all of creation. Through contemplation of the sacred trinity, bright soul, I invite you to explore the depths of divine mystery and embrace the interconnectedness of all existence.

Terra Speaks

Foster a sense of reverence and stewardship for the planet and all its inhabitants by embracing nature's trinities. You can start by observing the cycles of birth, growth, and decay in plants, animals, and ecosystems — acknowledging the trinity of creation, preservation, and transformation. Practising mindfulness in your interactions with nature will help you attune to the interplay of earth, water, and sky, symbolising the trinity of elements that sustain life. Additionally, you can cultivate a deeper connection to the natural world by celebrating the trinity of sun, moon, and stars, which govern the rhythms of day and night. By embracing these nature trinities in your daily life, little dragon, you align yourself with the inherent balance and harmony of the universe.

Umbra Growls

Enough with the harmful trinity of power, privilege, and prejudice! I'm sick of seeing inequality run rampant in humanity. Those in power cling to their privilege, while prejudice keeps others down. It's a vicious cycle that needs to be broken. Please do not sit idly by while injustice thrives. It's time to roar and demand change. It is time to dismantle systems that perpetuate inequality and uplift those who've been marginalised. Be fierce, human. Use your words to show your support. Use your actions to fight against this harmful trinity once and for all. Enough is enough.

Truth

Affirmation

I embrace the truth within and around me. With courage, I seek it, knowing it brings clarity and authenticity to my life. I trust in my ability to discern truth from falsehood, allowing honesty to guide my actions and decisions. I am empowered by the truth, for it aligns me with my deepest values and leads me towards genuine connection and growth.

Lux Shines

Bright soul, in this universe, the only truth is that nothing is permanent. Even truths you consider absolute are subject to change. Yes, it is an absolute truth that the sun rises in the east and sets in the west. It is an absolute truth that night follows day. It is an absolute truth that your beautiful, magical Gaia travels around the star Sol that sits at the centre of your galaxy. But these truths are only absolute in the here and now. Tomorrow is unwritten and may bring forth a cosmic calamity that alters these absolutes and creates a new truth. Truth only has a foundation in the present and the past. With increased knowledge, all truths can change. Accept this. Just because something was and is, it does not guarantee it will always be. Armed with this truth, look back and see that the person you are today is no longer the person you were just a year ago. See the truth of you in the present and let go of truths that no longer serve or honour the person you have become.

Terra Speaks

What is truth for you, little dragon, may not be true for another. This, as much as it may challenge you and cause upset, is why it is important to understand that your opinion is not necessarily correct. It is a subjective truth based on your thoughts, feelings, and experiences. Know that your thoughts and feelings are valid, and a truth that honours and serves you well is a truth to live by. Be authentic and embrace it. But it does you no honour to force others to live by your truth. Your truth is yours, and in living your truth, you show integrity. You shine. By walking your talk, you shine. Do not dull your light by expecting others to agree or do things your way. Sometimes, you will shine all the brighter because you create a space in which others can find their own truth on their way. That we must allow others to be and to become who they are meant to be on their own terms is a truth we must all eventually accept.

Umbra Growls

Something might appear true in a particular circumstance, but truth is not always fact. It is only a fact if a reliable source can verify it. Without verification, the information offered could be nought more than conjecture — i.e., founded on misinformation or only partial information. All too often, a bit of truth, sometimes factual truth, is wrapped up in a whole lot of lies to create a scenario that appears plausible and genuine. This is almost pure fabrication, crafted to fool and mislead. Human, don't be stubborn. Do not allow arrogance to close your mind. Do not allow your biases to make you believe something is true when the facts say otherwise. Yes, the truth might make you uncomfortable, but it's better to be uncomfortable for a moment than believe in a lie that may lead you, or those you love, to harm.

Acknowledgements

I would like to thank the following people for being a part of my crazy world and playing a key role in my creative journey:

Blue Angel Publishing: As always, you have given me the space and freedom to create. I am forever grateful and appreciative.

My patrons, past and present: Thank you for helping to keep me creating and your incredible patience. You are treasured — Anthea Wright, Lauren Sarlya, Nick Gronlund, Alana Jones, Connie Morrighan, Deborah R. Moore, Barbara Espinel, Beverley Baines, Theresa Neveau, Mary Lou Stevens, Auroras Light, Igor Chuprov, Katye Mitchell, Alexandra Boadicée, Sharon, Bernadette Fugier, Lynda Ferrell, Beth Turner, Jordan Lynn Gribble, Celina McMahon, Taryn, Ashley Bryner, Carrie Anais, Martin Calderwood, Kym Pearce, Bobbie Powe, Marla Hill, Kat Reynolds, Amariel Panacea, Jennifer Martin, Danielle Evans, Pania Harris, Lynn E Palmer, Trin Achronism, Steven Klimecky, Kerrie Rusk, Sharon Promnitz, Alexandra Rena, Amy Brown, Andrea Wills, Louisa Dent, Isabel Draken, Chris Nash, Heather Willis, Trisha Fant, Kelly Fitzgerald, Hayley Anderson, Karen Williams, Sunny Wang, Jenny Mitchell, Jenny Amos, Olivia Gross, Sharlene Sexton, Carole Woolcock, Jenelle Hotson, Kyliejean Pearn, Emma Bolton, Tracey Anderson.

About the Creator

RAVYNNE PHELAN is an internationally recognised and bestselling artist and creator. Her titles include *Messenger Oracle*, *Dreams of Dragons & Dragon Kin Colouring Book*, *Dreams of Magic*, the award-winning *Dreams of Gaia Tarot*, *Dreams of Gaia Tarot Pocket Edition*, *Ravynne Phelan's Spirit Animal Colouring Book*, and *Seeker Oracle*.

To learn more about Ravynne and her work, visit **www.ravynnephelan.com**

Also available from Blue Angel Publishing®

SEEKER ORACLE
Ravynne Phelan

A seeker suspects there is something more ... in the quiet of sunrise, the song of night and the overlapping folds of our present, our beyond, and our world. They are curious, not just for who they are, but for who they can become. The seeker finds wisdom in the wonderful, possibility in the peculiar, and treasure in the strange and the mundane. They recognise themselves in the mirror of time, place and creature, and for them, the accrual of knowledge is a consistent consequence of every experience.

Seeker Oracle is for the inquisitive, the questioning, and those ready not just for greener pastures but for forsaken forests, overlooked woodlands, and technicoloured timberland. Your 55 fantastical companions will walk with you, share their insight, and nudge you further along your exquisite journey of discovery.

ISBN: 978-1-922573-12-4
55 cards + 136-page guidebook

Also available from Blue Angel Publishing®

DREAMS OF GAIA TAROT

Ravynne Phelan

A Tarot for a New Era

The philosophy of the *Dreams of Gaia Tarot* is simple: to seek, to feel, to grow, to heal. This deck will strengthen your connection to your divine self, whilst helping you to identify and heal past experiences that hold you back from living to your fullest potential.

By offering structure in the form of a major and minor arcana like that of past tarots, but combining them with bold new archetypes, symbology, and meanings more suited to the present, the *Dreams of Gaia Tarot* allows for a more personal, intimate, and effective system for using cards as a roadmap to navigate your life path. Embark on this extraordinary journey of undoing, of being, and becoming, and be inspired by the knowledge that all that manifests in your future is born of choices you make today.

ISBN: 978-1-922161-95-6
81 cards + 308-page guidebook

Also available from Blue Angel Publishing®

RAVYNNE PHELAN'S SPIRIT ANIMAL COLORING BOOK

Ravynne Phelan

The magic and medicine of color and the wonder of animals great and small come together in this delightsome offering from beloved artist and author Ravynne Phelan.

Release your creativity and deepen your connections with the animal world as you bring the majesty, mischief, and grace of the wild to life. Meet Fire Fox, Ghost Cat, Storm Falcon, and more fantastic creatures from the skies, oceans, gardens, and forests of the world. The 50 lineworks are based on original drawings and paintings with some much-loved images you are sure to recognize along with others created especially for this collection.

ISBN: 978-1-925538-84-7
104 pages, paperback.

Also available from Blue Angel Publishing®

THE MESSENGER'S SCRIBE
Writing & Creativity Journal
Ravynne Phelan

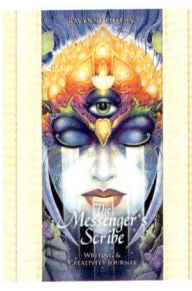

Commune with the Messengers and know your heart.

Open like a flower to the song of life and the magic that surrounds and flows through all. Acknowledge, reaffirm, understand, and celebrate your connection with Gaia. This journal holds sacred space. It is free of judgement and blossoming with a loving invitation to liberate, release, and express all you are meant to be. The Messengers you find within these pages are your trusted companions. Speak with them, for they will show you the way …

ISBN: 978-1-922573-92-6
220-page deluxe journal.

Notes

Notes

www.BlueAngelOnline.com